My Life During the "Winds of Change"

By

Eldon Mackridge

Eldon J. Mackridge
Feb 13th 2024.

Published by New Generation Publishing in 2021

Copyright © Eldon Mackridge 2021

First Edition

The author asserts the moral right under the Copyright, Designs and Patents Act 1988 to be identified as the author of this work.

All Rights reserved. No part of this publication may be reproduced, stored in a retrieval system or transmitted, in any form or by any means without the prior consent of the author, nor be otherwise circulated in any form of binding or cover other than that which it is published and without a similar condition being imposed on the subsequent purchaser.

ISBN 978-1-80031-180-0

www.newgeneration-publishing.com

New Generation Publishing

Introduction

A story of Eldon James Mackridge's life starting in South London during World War Two. Being forced out of his family home in London by Hitler. Experiences in Norfolk with local relatives, country folk and American airmen. Struggling with school work. Returning home to post war South London. The joys of being a choirboy, cub scout, newspaper boy, and keen cyclist. First job as an engineering apprentice, before joining the British Army and travelling overseas to Libya and Kenya which was a great education in its self. Returning to the UK to become a Personnel Manager, a Special Constable for two Counties and Clerk to local parishes councils. Forming his own company, and then ending up as a self-employed chauffeur. Experiences as a Freemasonry. Then retirement and being honoured with the Freedom of the Town of Haverhill, Suffolk.

Eldon James Mackridge born 8th September, 1937

**Life during the
"Winds of Change"**

Second World War

Now the start of that life. I was born into a world amid war, destruction and confusion not knowing any other life until I was eight years old. We all have childhood memories. One of my first was collecting shrapnel and chaff (aluminium foil which was released from German aircraft to upset our radar), on my way to school. These were great items to swap and build up a collection. Helping mum, (Edith May Mackridge born 22nd Feb. 1901 the same date that Queen Victoria died. My mum died December 1970) to put washing on the line and hearing gun fire in the distance. Seeing fighter aircraft flying round and round over our house. Although I have these isolated memories before Wednesday 21st June 1944 it was on this day that my memory in life started nearly continuously with small gaps. My Father, James Frederick Mackridge born 22nd January 1905, died 25th December 1986, was enlisted on 22nd April 1942 into the army RASC (Royal Army Service Corps). He was called for military service later in the war due to his age. He was serving in Italy and advancing northwards at this time. I have fond memories of my father practising rifle drill in the kitchen

with a broom stick before he went abroad in 1943. He worked at St Guys Hospital London all his working life. Most people in those days worked for the same employer all their working life unless some unforeseen circumstances arose.

V1 & V2 logs SE25 South Norwood

Next area : SE27

PostCode	Borough	Type	Area	Position	Deaths	Date	Time	Notes
SE25	Croydon	V1	South Norwood	Junction Warminster Road and Avenue Road	1	15/06/1944	05:07	V1 struck Warminster Road the first to fall in the Borough of Croydon 5 houses were demolished and 30 severely damaged.
SE25	Croydon	V1	Selhurst	St James Road and Selhurst new road	7	17/06/1944	02:40	V1 in Selhurst New Road demolished 7 houses and caused severe blast damage to surroundings
SE25	Croydon	V1	Upper Norwood	North West side of Ross Road	2	21/06/1944 (wednesday)	14:52	V1 in Ross Road . There is a very detailed Croydon Borough Engineers report for the incident which reports "Demolished 36,38,40,22,44 Ross Road and 45 Falkland Park Avenue 32,34,46,48 Ross Road and 37,39,41,43,47,49,51,53 Falkland Park Avenue unstable 24-30 & 50-58 19,21,33,35 Ross Road and 25-35 55 57 59 42-50 Falkland Park Avenue seriously damaged. Blast damage across 1/4 mile radius" It is of interest that the Blast damage in Ross Road and Falkland Park Avenue is undetectable as the Houses were rebuilt in the same style as their Neighbours

I was at Cypress Road Primary School when we were all sent to the air raid shelters in the basement by our teachers, the air raid siren was sounding at 14:40 hours on Wednesday 21st June 1944. I was really scared stiff. An older girl sitting opposite me said out loud pointing at me "Look at that little boy, he looks really frightened", I was really frightened. From the records a V1 flying bomb had exploded at the north west side of Ross Road, the road to rear of our house, and about five houses to the west. The blast caused damage across a quarter of a mile radius. My mother managed to get Jasmine, my younger sister, aged 4, into our Morrison shelter in the front room and was just getting herself in the shelter, when the blast blew the door of the room off its hinges and hit Mum on her back. She complained about her back pains for years after the war. A Morrison Shelter, was named after Herbert Morrison the Home Secretary in 1941. It was a big steel table, that a family could sleep under at night in safety in case of an air raid and have meals sitting around it during the day. However, the Anderson shelter on the other hand was constructed from corrugated steel and buried underground in the garden. Named after Sir John Anderson who in 1938 was responsible for preparing Britain to withstand German air raids.

The Weekly family who lived at No. 39 had an Anderson shelter, and we played in this shelter after the war. At all times we carried with us gas masks in the event of a gas attack, Jasmine being a young child had a Mickey Mouse type. A gas attack never happened which I am pleased to say, because the gas masks were not very pleasant equipment for children to wear. Wearing them during an exercise was horrible experience. I would break the seal at the side of my face and suck in fresh air to breath easily.

After the all clear sounded we were sent home. On the way home I met my older sister, Heather who is two years older than me.

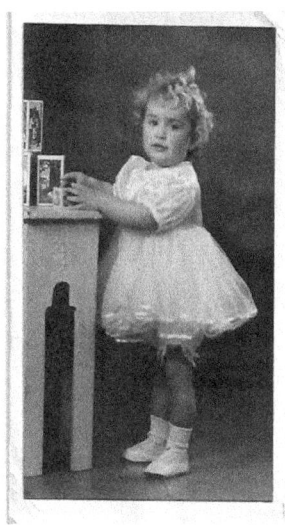

As we approached Falkland Park Avenue, where we lived, we became aware that a V1 bomb had damaged many houses. The first V1 flying rocket fell on London in the Woolwich area on the morning of 13th June 1944) They had nick names such as "Buzz Bombs" or "Doodlebugs" and were the first type of cruise missile. A man named Robert Lusser invented them. The first V2 (German: Vergeitungswaffe 2) to hit London on 8th September, 1944 was the world's first long range guided ballistic missile that entered space before returning to earth with terrible destruction.

As we ran up the Avenue, we seemed more interested to see if the translucent glass fanlight with the number 35 over the front door was broken on our house than all the destruction around us. War and destruction must have been common place to us, in those days, because we knew of no other life. The avenue was in utter chaos. A lady recognised us and took us to a house, that was slightly damaged, where our mother and younger sister, Jasmine, were drinking tea. During the war neighbours were very caring. We were on speaking terms with nearly all the residents in the area. I can still remember the surnames of those living around us, the next-door neighbours were called "aunt and uncle", they were Mr & Mrs Jamieson who were Scottish and members of the Salvation Army. Their house was owned by the Salvation Army and Mr Jamieson worked for the Army full time at their Insurance Offices in London. On the other side lived a retired couple Mr & Mrs Gap. Mr Gap was a retired London bus driver. Opposite lived Mr & Mrs Symonds, he was a scientist. We could not stay at our bombed-out house because it was unstable so Mum took us to her sister's house.

Mum's sister, Aunt Vera Horlock, lived at New Malden. I can remember boarding a trolleybus at South Norwood Junction and the clippie asking mum for the fare. Mum stated that we had just been bombed out and she had no money or belongings on or about her. London Transport let us travel free of charge. A trolleybus was propelled by electricity which was obtained from two overhead wires. In later life it amazed me how this system continued with power being generated somewhere in London and distributed all over the routes without too damage. If it was damaged there must have been a fear of people being electrocuted, but I trust a "fail safe" system was built into the overhead wires system.

We spent one night at New Malden with our Uncle Alan, Aunt Vera Horlock and our cousin Felicity. During the night there was an air raid attack some distance away, and in the morning Uncle Alan was annoyed about a cracked windowpane. I thought to myself, big deal we've lost our whole house. We travelled to Bunwell in Norfolk by bus and train. I remember the train stopping in the Ipswich area when children were told to hide under the seats. German aircraft or flying bombs were overhead. We got off the train at Tivetshall station Norfolk. Mum had organised a local Austin taxi driven by a Miss Thurston to take us to Bunwell Low Common.

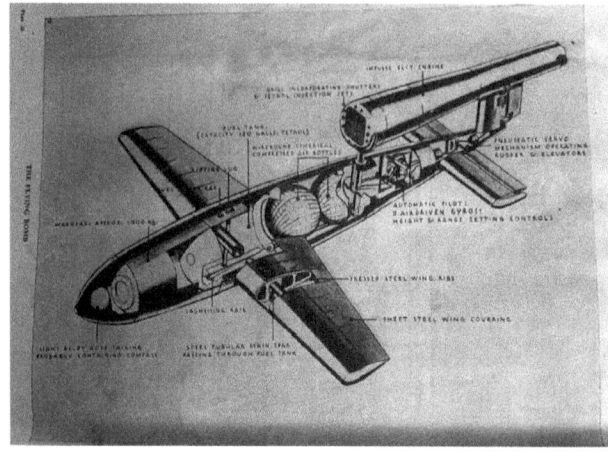

This was my second time in Norfolk during the war. My first period was during the so-called phoney War from 3rd September 1939 to 10th May 1940 when we lived at Park Farm, Low Common, Bunwell with a Great Aunt Grace and Great Uncle Harry Smith, and their son "little" Harry Smith. After the Blitz and Battle of Britain we came back to Falkland Park Avenue to be bombed out after this so called 'phoney war'.

I have the odd memory during this period living at Park Farm.

One was seeing an elderly lady Mrs Marianne Rivett plucking a small bird in the kitchen, this lady must have been Aunt Grace Smith's mother and she was either visiting or living at Park Farm. There was also a maid called Evelyn Humphreys, who worked in the milking parlour. If we were good Evelyn would allow us into the parlour to watch the milk being cooled in the cooling machine. Evelyn was like one of the family as she did some of the housework and looked after us. Many years after the war when we visited Park Farm, Evelyn was still there, and as young teenagers she reacted with us as a great friend. Evelyn was very insular and knowing we came from London asked me one day if I had ever seen the Queen on a daily basis. Evelyn may have eventually married Little Harry I have been lead to believe. It is hard for people these days to understand that country folk never travelled far from their homesteads. Uncle Harry was born at Park Farm, lived and worked his whole life there and died in the same bed he was born in, except for a short period during the First World War. Little Harry, (born 2nd July 1933 died 2nd March 1994) also, was born and died at Park Farm. It was the same my father-in-law, William Shinn, a gamekeeper / forester was well travelled in a sort of way. In his early working life, he travelled from job to job in East Anglia / Lincolnshire, but never any further. I took him to London once and had a feeling that it was his first and maybe only trip to the capital. The difference between country and town folk was notable in all parts of England, or maybe the world. The accents throughout the British Isles always interested me, when I joined the forces, it was a culture shock to hear the way people spoke. Not only that, different nouns and adjectives were used in the English language. It didn't dawn on me that northerners thought southern folk spoke with a funny accent too.

Life as an "evacuee" in Norfolk for the second time

Bunwell cottages 1920's

Taken during the War 1943

Picture taken 2019

I would like to mention that we were not official evacuees, because we had relations in Norfolk, and a safe place away from the bombing. My Grandmother let us have a cottage at Valley Farm, Bridge Road, Lower Common Bunwell. The cottage was the middle cottage in a row of three set at right angles to the road. Grandma lived in the left and in the cottage to the right lived a Mr & Mrs Warren and their son Percy who was about my age. I have a recent photograph of the cottages and it still appears exactly as they were during the war. Of course, there wasn't any bathroom or running water which was obtained from a hand pump situated outside of the three cottages. Bath time was good fun, in a portable zinc bath in front of the living room fire. The water was heated in a copper; (the copper was a large up turned copper dome fixed over brickwork where a fire was lit underneath) in the kitchen using coal or wood. When the water was hot enough it was ladled into the via zinc bath in the living room.   After bath time it was emptied in the back yard and hang on the wall outside. However, we did have mains electricity with one light in each room and only one plug in the living room.   Mum used this single electrically socket to the capacity with multi extensions.

My Grandfather Charles Tunmore born March 1863, died 9th March 1938, and Edith his wife born 22nd October 1867 and died in 1949, lived in Kennington, Lambeth, London before retiring to Bunwell. Charles Tunmore was a carpenter and specialised in the manufacture and the fitting of large public houses in London. He worked in conjunction with a glass and mirror dealer called Mr. Quartermaine. Mr Quartermaine's daughter, Grace, was my God mother. She gave me a solid silver serviette or napkin ring hallmarked made Birmingham 1934 when I was christened, which I still have. My grandparents may have owned many cottages in England, because I remember collecting rent at a later stage in my life with my mother. It seems that when my maternal grandad retired, they moved back to Bunwell and Aslacton areas where they were born. The Tunmore family in fact came from Aslacton a few miles from Bunwell. I have yet to research this branch of the Tunmore family in depth.   The nearest working Farm House to us in Bunwell was Ruby Farm, which was farmed and owned by Mr & Mrs Stimpson (whose apples I scrummed from their huge orchards), The Stimpson children were named: - Alec, Nancy, Leonard, Peter and Ruby. Nancy told me off once when I uttered a word that I had learnt from other boys at Bunwell school. Nancy said she did not like little boys who swore. I didn't realise "bugger" was a naughty word and felt ashamed of myself and never swore again.

One morning I was walking up Bridge Road to Ruby Farm to get the milk. (We collected milk every day in a two-pint enamelled vessel from this farm). One day I looked up to the sky and saw an aircraft pulling another aircraft without engines. This I was told later, was a D-Day or "Operation Overlord" landing Glider being pulled by a nylon rope, I thought nylons were stockings that US airman gave to young ladies. This took me some time to work out. The British gliders were "Airspeed Horsman" for carrying troops or Sherman tanks. Both the Allies and Germans used this form of glider to land troops on land they were fighting for.

My mother was given some baby chickens by a local farmer. They grew into good egg producers, and it was a daily job to collect these eggs before getting ready for the walk to school during the laying season. Some eggs were saved and preserved in "liquid glass" which was a clear syrup looking substance that sealed the egg shell to prevent the inner egg turning bad. This liquid glass was very handy to use as an adhesive, for example mum even used it to stick tiles back on to the kitchen walls that had falling off due to bad workmanship.

During this period, I learnt to ride a bicycle, with the help of the Stimpson boys. This put me in good stead for the future, as I came a very keen cyclist in later years.

We formed great friends with the Stimpson children and walked to Bunwell School and back with them, which was about two miles each way. In the summer months we could take a short cut across the fields. We loved picking the kale and eating it as we walked home. My Grandma told me that my Great Uncle Eldon James Smith was a Builder/Contractor/Farmer and had built Bunwell School amongst many others in the area. I did not really believe her, but in later years my children found out this was true, and I was named after him. This Eldon James Smith was a brother of my Grandma. She was a Smith before she married my maternal grandad, Charles Tunmore. On studying this branch of the Smith family tree there were many men named "Eldon James" during the 18th to 20th centuries.

I can't remember my first days at Bunwell School. This is strange, because I would have thought that a new environment would have stuck in my memory. No doubt the memory of starting at a new school was overshadowed by having witnessed being bombed out of home and the upheaval of our family. My Mother must have been brave to endure losing her house whilst her husband was away and still dealing three young children. There were three classrooms at Bunwell School, Miss Yellow taught me in the infant's room, Mrs Humphrey was in charge of the Junior class, where my sister Heather was, and the Head Master Mr. Douglas taught the older children before they left school to face life. I did not have any problems with the local children at school. I believe some evacuees had unhappy times and wanted to go back to London. There was only one other boy in the class from London as far as I can remember. I had local relations and friends from the Farms in the area and was sort of accepted as local. During my research I discovered there were many more evacuees than I thought, also extra teachers posted to Bunwell school from the east of London. My worst experience was when the school was being repainted and I leant on a freshly painted black water down pipe that left a big black stripe down my clean grey school jersey and shorts. I was laughed at by the other students. My mum was not too pleased when I got home that afternoon. This must have given her many more hours washing with hot water in the copper. We spent most of the summer months playing out in the fields.

    The farm workers also joined the local Home Guard and one great memory of mine was seeing a platoon parading in Bridge Road, with a dog running loose in and out of the ranks, with much annoyance to the squad and officer in charge. (This memory was relieved when the same thing happened to me, while I was in the army during my African tour, a feral dog running in and out of the ranks during morning parade). Harvest time was very special, watching the old Allis Chalmer tractors and binder cut the corn and bind it into sheaves, for the farm workers to stand the sheaves up to form stooks. When the corn had dried it was ready to be moved to the threshing yard at the farm. We then rode on top of a tumble (four wheeled cart) load of sheaf's pulled by horses to the thrashing yard. A great day was had by all when a steam threshing machine came to Ruby Farm to thrash the corn. At this stage of the war horses were still being used as much as possible on the farms to save petrol. The threshing machine attached to a steam engine was hired out to farms by contractors. This experience of watching the corn being trashed was one of my highlights as a young boy. Seeing the farm hands working very hard, the driving belts flapping about, the external wheels whirling around, steam, smoke, fire, dust and the sacks of corn being filled, and taken to the barn. The straw was then built up by pitchforks to form a hay stack. There were no health and safety restrictions in those days, so unguarded belts, wheels and dust plus lack of safety clothing were all the order of the day. In retrospect I think we were sent to be with the farmworkers during the school holidays because we were looked after, in a kind of way, and did not get into trouble, plus our parents knew where we were. Local children were learning the farm trade from a very young age and helping a bit due to a man shortage. Farmworkers had a very short life due to the dust, unhealthy working conditions and dangerous mechanical farm implements.

Combine harvesters had been invented in USA at this time but were not in common use in Britain until after the 1950's. I remember seeing one of the first combine harvesters working in the field near to Uncle Kenny Smith's butchers' shop at Forncett End well after the war. It was a very small machine with no cabin or air conditioning compared with those of today. A farmer's wife, Doris Brown, a younger sister of my grandma, who lived at Church Farm, Carlton Rode came to see us occasionally at Low Common driving a pony and trap. This was to save running her car and using her petrol coupons. One day she collected us and our Grandma from Bunwell Low Common and took us all over to Church Farm Carleton Rode for Sunday tea. It was a great experience the wind in our hair and the sound of the pony's hoofs. On the return trip Aunt Doris sat chatting to Grandma and Mum, the pony knew the way. (One day cars will do this). Doris and her husband Percy Brown had two boys, Maurice and Trevor. One day at Church Farm Carleton Rode I had my first experience of meeting true gypsies, Percy Brown had allowed them to park their horse drawn caravan on one of his fields. We made friends with them and learnt how they lived in the caravan, which seemed very exciting to us children. One gypsy made me a pea shooter made from a hollowed-out cane and part of a clock spring. By pulling on the bent clock spring the pea was propelled out of the cane at great speed. Great fun. Wooden toys were in short supply due to the fact that most wood was imported and wanted for the war effort. There wasn't any plastic or the earlier Bakelite, sometimes spelt Bakelite named after the inventor/chemist a Belgian-American called Leo Baekeland, because it had not been invented until the early 1900's. Thank goodness. I remember after the war being given a miniature camera made out of Bakelite which was my first contact with such a material. During the late 1960's the other material, "plastic" really came into our lives. Mother made a toy pram for my youngest sister Jasmine, out of an old wooden delivery box. The pram was constructed by fixing a handle made from three pieces of one-inch x half inch wood nailed to the top open end of the box. The four wheels were made of square pieces of wood nailed to the bottom end, which mum cut the corners off then cut the eight points to resemble almost circular wheels. Then, finally, got Jasmine to push the pram up and down the road outside the house until the wheels were roughly worn round. Life was really idyllic for us, away from the bombing in London and it all added to my general education. Travel in its self was a great education my mum always impressed on us.

However, we were not totally away from the war because there were many military airfields all around us which could attract enemy bombing at any time. There were about 38 military airfields in Norfolk made up from RAF, RN and US Army Air Forces. The nearest airfields to Bunwell were Tibenham and Old Buckingham and further afield East Wretham, Hethel and Deopham Green. On the way to school nearly every morning we saw bombers returning from raids over Germany with two or more engines idol and fuselages shot up. These Bombers were mainly Boeing B-17 Flying Fortresses crewed by 10 men of an average age of 22 years. The other type of bomber was the Consolidated Liberator. There were often loud explosions when bombers hit the ground on landing. The noise was so loud sometimes to shake the bed early in the morning and wake us up for school. (like an alarm clock). During the war we had a double summer time, meaning the clocks were put forward TWO hours. In the summer time it was 11:15pm before it was completely dark, and I lay in bed until the late hours listening to bombers taking off from nearby airfields and forming into groups above for bombing raids over Germany. You can imagine there were many American airmen in the area and we had great fun calling to them as they passed on cycles or Jeeps, "Have you got any gum chum". A US Airman on a bicycle stopped, one afternoon, while I was on my way home from school and gave me some gum and asked where I lived. He said jump up on to my cross bar I'll give you a lift home. I was a bit worried if he knew where Bridge Road, Low Common was, but all went well. On reaching home, my mother was at the garden Gate. The airman held out his hand full of coins and said help yourself son (I can still see it as if it was yesterday). Not appearing to be greedy I took a penny. Come on son have half a crown. I thanked him as he cycled off. 2/6d in those days was a lot of money, mum told me to share it with my two sisters. Multiply 12.5p by 12 and you get an idea of the estimated value: - £1.50 in today's money. I always wondered why this airman stopped to give me a lift home and seemed to know where I lived, and more strangely that my mum was at the back gate to our house to greet me home.

Around about Christmas time, United States airman arrived at the school in big army lorries with four airmen in the back of each truck for safety to take us to their airfield base. We had a really good American party. I think our teachers were worried that we might get lost, so we all formed a circle by joining hands around the younger children, so they and us would not get mixed up with other school parties. The Christmas Trees looked huge. We came home sick as dogs due to the rich American food and drinks like Coca-Cola, which was all new to us and buns with some sticky sweet stuff that we had never seen before. I think the Americans made a fuss of us because they were away from their families and missed seeing their own little children.

The Americans were really good fun and joined in with the local Church fêtes and village fairs on the village green behind the school. I was really infatuated by the US airmen, they seemed so rich, had great looking uniforms and were very generous. The older teenage girls were also attracted to them. It was not unusual to see girls walking hand in hand with American airman, or riding in their Jeeps. I understand that some girls eventually married the young airman and went to the United States as G.I. brides.

I was not a good scholar at school. However, Miss Yellow taught me how to knit with white string, plain knit and cast off, until the string was nearly black due to my young sweaty little hands. I was very proud that at least I could do something, although I could not still write or do sums very well. The older boys and girls in the class sat at the back of the large classroom and were always being told off for passing written notes to each other. I was told by my companions they were love letters. What that meant, I was still in the dark.

My father sent my sister an Italian doll from Italy. My mother told my sister and me to go down Bridge Road to Heather Farm where Italian prisoners of war were helping with farm work and ascertain an Italian name for the doll. The prisoners were very friendly and gave us a list of names. The prisoners were all dressed in a dark brown working uniforms with badges so they could easily be recognised. There were also German prisoners of war, working on some farms but they had less freedom. Years later when I was a Personnel Manager at Whitlock Bros. Great Yeldham, Essex one of the workers was an ex-German prisoner of war who was known as Herman the German. He told me that he decided to remain working on a farm in England after the war because the English way of life appealed to him.

We were constantly reminded that a war was on, because of those bombers flying overhead constantly. I didn't remember seeing any fighter aircraft, I guess they were stationed elsewhere. The small roads especially the Turnpike where Bunwell School and Villa were located was full of moving military transport. British Army Bedford fuel tankers, American army lorries and Queen Mary trailers, which were long trailers specially manufactured to carry parts of aircraft fuselage or wings, were constantly passing us on the narrow roads. The Turnpike near Bunwell school and the Villa has now been diverted and widened.

Returning to London SE25

When the War ended in Europe, we still lived in Norfolk for some time before moving back to South Norwood. One evening Uncle Alan took Gerald Smith and me to Norwich Speed Way in his Austin 8 which was his company car. We had a good time cheering on Split Waterman a famous rider, our hero at the time. On our return Mum put me in the zinc bath tub, I was full of cinders that were sprayed on Gerald and me as the riders went round the bend where we were standing. We all moved for a few months to live with my paternal grandparents in the St. Albans area before returning to Falkland Park Avenue. My Grandfather had been  helping my mother with belongings saved from our bombed house as my father was still in the Army and did not return home until some date in 1946. My Grandfather, James Mackridge, born in 1876 & Grandma, Ethel nee Purser, also born 1876 lived at 3, Firwood Avenue. Their daughter, Aunt Effie Hancock, and her husband, Uncle Ted Hancock, with their two boys, David and Ray, lived in the semidetached next door that is: - 1, Firwood Avenue Colney Heath St. Albans, Hertfordshire. Uncle Ted Hancock worked at de Havilland aircraft factory during WW 1 and 2. He was basically a carpenter because the first aircraft were manufacture out of wood. He went with the de Havilland family to Canada in the 1920/30's to help set up a factory somewhere in Canada.

I can remember on 15th August 1945 VE celebrations were held further down Firwood Avenue. This was with the burning of a crashed de Havilland Mosquito bonfire. As the DH Mosquito aircraft were constructed of mostly wood, there was a grand display of flames. The grownups were dancing and kissing one another, peace meant more to them, than us children. A life of bombs, guns and aircraft overhead was the only life I knew, not peace. The war against Japan ended on 2nd September 1945, VJ day. At the time I did not know that the Americans dropped atomic bombs on Japan. This fact was not general knowledge to us children. I eventually realised about this great event in my early teens.

My paternal grandfather James Mackridge had an interesting life, he served an indentured apprenticeship, working as an engineer on a private steam yacht. Later he lived in the mews working as a chauffeur/mechanical engineer to a rich family in Mill Hill, North London. I have a photograph of him at the wheel of a car taken about the1880's. My father was born and lived at this address until he married my mother. During the second World War my grandfather worked at the de Havilland aircraft factory Hatfield when he was living at Colney Heath, St. Albans, Hertfordshire.

On settling back in to our rebuilt home during 1946 at Falkland Park Avenue, everything seemed about the same. We soon begun to meet up with the children we knew before the blitz and bombing and played with them in the Avenue. There weren't many vehicles about so it was quite safe. The war damage re-building scheme had given us a new house with a fresh undercoat on the woodwork. My Dad glossed the woodwork when he was demobilised. I can remember the day he came home it was about early 1947. We woke one morning and he was there, he must have had arrived home after we went to asleep. It was a great day, Great Aunt Tot Storey real name Sarah nee Purser was staying with us and joined in the celebrations of Dad being with us again after the war. Father worked at Guy's Hospital near London Bridge nearly all his working life except for a short period at St. Thomas Hospital and while he was in the Army during World War 2. That's what people did then. My younger sister, Jasmine who was born 8th March 1940 did not remember our Dad and said to Mum, "When is that man going to go away". My Mum had six chickens and one duck (who was called Donald) in the garden for extra eggs. The rationing of food continued well after the end of hostilities. My Godmother Grace Quartermaine lived in Wincott Street Kennington adjacent to Kennington Road, Lambeth SE11 where my maternal grandparents lived prior to moving to Bunwell Low Common in 1938/9. Aunt Grace Quartermaine visited us on a regular basis at Falkland Park Avenue. I was sent back to Cypress Road Primary School until my eleven plus exam. Here again my past memory is a bit sketchy during my return to Cypress Road, but I can remember a girl called Molly sitting near to me, perhaps I was getting her mixed up with

"Milly Molly Mandy" by Joyce Lankester Brisley. At Christmas times we made a Paper Father Christmas's. I cannot even remember the teacher's name. I have a very faint recollection that her name was Miss Arrow, but I cannot guarantee this. She tried to get me to read on a one-to-one basis at her desk, the only word I recognised once was "luncheon". "How do you know that word" she said, I replied. "I saw it in windows of guest houses when I was on holiday at Margate. We were taught the poems by William Shakespeare, one of these was: - "Where the bee sucks, there suck I. In a cowslip's bell I lie". From "Tempest"). My father tried to help me read by reading the narrative of "Rupert the Bear" which was published in the "Daily Express" newspaper each day. He, also, read a story to us children at bedtime and encouraged me to follow the words as he read the written word out loud.

I thought it was very bad form of the Head Master, when seeing me in the corridor one day and saying, "You've got your Eleven Plus Exam tomorrow, you won't pass but look at the questions". He was right I could not even read the examination papers let alone complete any answers, so I was sent to an all-boys school called Ingram Road Secondary Modern School in September 1948. I was the youngest in the class due my birthday being in September. I soon made friends with the other boys and settled down to the routine. Whist I attended at secondary school the Korean War commenced and ended: i.e., June 1950 until 1953. My Mother sent me to elocution lessons and tap-dancing lessons at the Patricia Ash school of dancing in Auckland Road. In a funny way I enjoyed this and met a chap called Trevor Wright. We were the only boys at the classes we attended, so you can imagine we were great heroes with all the girls. I also, joined a cub pack, in, uniform for the first time. The 48th Beckenham pack that met in a bombed-out basement of a house in Auckland Road. Then later the pack met at St Johns the Evangelist Church Hall. One Christmas the cub pack organised a production of Charles Dickens "A Christmas Carol". I was selected to play "Tiny Tim" the sentence I had to learn was: - "God bless us everyone". I remember a lot of clapping, so guess it was OK. I never proceeded to be a scout because my choirboy and other commitments were too great. However, Akela, Baloo and Bagheera the pack leaders were very good, and taught us the scouting code, we attended church parades and learnt marching and simple drill, which was handy for when I joined the Army.

Something remarkable happened a few months after starting at Ingram Road Secondary School, I began to be bit of a scholar. I had been what you call a slow learner or late developer. I really enjoyed religious instruction and science, mainly because I learnt a lot of religion at church and I was very interested in science. The Science master was Mr Lawson, I understood him and what he was teaching. He gave me science homework and I made a good job of underlining the headings were: - Method, Experiment, Conclusion and Result in coloured inks. What with a paper round, Cubs, choir boy, cycling, elocution lessons and tap dancing lessons, I was a of very busy boy.

My Mother was a character, she had been hard of hearing since birth and always made up what she didn't hear. However, she always judged people on meeting them and afterwards liked to have discussions regarding their station in life. We had fun regarding other people's class in life, in her words; a stiff upper lip, no back bone or lethargic etc. She was a bit of a snob, and always said I had blue blood in my veins. During my upbringing the class system was more defined than it is now. The working class knew their place, labourers etc. Skilled artisans were the bottom of the middle class and doctors, teacher, police officers and those who had attended Oxford or Cambridge University's etc. were half way up the ladder, lastly the upper classes were the Lords and Ladies that owned large areas of land and stately houses.

Mother would always insist that we had a holiday, other than the first holiday after the war at Margate with our great aunts, the venues later were Shanklin, Isle of Wight, Gorleston on Sea, Yarmouth, Hopton in Norfolk. We mainly hired houses except one year at Yarmouth, we had the luxury of a hotel. Holidays consisted mainly of playing on the beach, walking miles, and eating ice cream. We visited a relation who owned an electrical supply shop in Yarmouth he and his wife lived in Hopton they had a posh car which was a large pre-war Armstrong Siddeley. Dad quite often cashed a cheque for £5 with this relation, he must have run out of cash half way through the holidays. There were no cash machines or other means of obtaining cash in those days. Fathers first car after the war was a 1934 Austin Seven, and as petrol was still rationed, he didn't use the car too much during the year. This was to conserve fuel so we had enough fuel coupons for a holiday. He didn't even use the car whilst on holiday, he would find a rented lock up garage to leave the car until our return trip. One bonus of going to Norfolk was to call in to see Uncle Alan Smith at Forncett St. Peter. Norfolk. Uncle Alan worked in the motor trade and seemed to always have petrol stored in his garage and he topped up Dad's tank every time we called in to see him. Just for interest, petrol cost about three shillings a gallon, 15 pence in today's money and road fund licence was £8.00.

Because my father worked at Guy's Hospital, we were fortunate enough to receive free medical treatment, which was a great bonus and a boost to my Mum's ego. In 1946 the NHS was formed so we were transferred to the Health Service. Guy's Hospital had, and still has, a dental school. We therefore had all our dental work carried out at Guy's by students, I remember travelling from home either by bus or train to Guy's Hospital for dental treatment on these occasions.

On returning from a shopping trip one day with my mother, passing a telephone exchange, it started to rain really hard.

"Quick," she said, "climb up into this parked GPO van for shelter". In those days' vehicles didn't always have locking doors. I sat there very worried, hoping the driver would not return. "Don't worry", my mother said, "it's a public service vehicle, we part own it!".

My mother would have liked me to take holy orders and become a vicar, but I'm afraid I disappointed her.

As a choirboy at St. Johns' Church Upper Norwood SE 19 I became a good soprano and attended all the Church Services, i.e., Holy Communion, Eucharist, and Evensong every Sunday. This was my first chance to dress up and play the character of a choirboy, into uniform for the second time. I learnt a tremendous amount of Christianity including the stations of the cross etc. I was Confirmed at quite a young age. and was always top in Religious Instruction at school. This gave me a little more confidence with my schooling. St. John the Evangelist at the junction of Auckland Road and Sylvan Road was bombed during the war. In the early days we only used the north aisle for services. I remember when the rest of the church had been rebuilt and was ready for worship again, Father Eric Bailey, the vicar, informed the congregation that it would

cost the church £100 to demolish the dividing temporary wall so the church could be complete again. The church seemed huge it is cathedral size. It was built when the Crystal Palace was moved to it's present position from Hyde Park. Many Victorian houses of rich families were built in the area. which needed a large place of worship. As a choirboy I listened to many sermons from our own priests as well as visiting clergymen. Us choirboys had a system of playing cricket with their words. I cannot explain it exactly but it was counting words that were repeated. When the banns were read out, "I hereby announce the marriage of Mr….. and Miss…. of this Parish. If anyone knows any cause or justice, why these persons should not be joined together in holy matrimony hereby declare it". We would then search the congregation for a young couple holding hands, or looking sweetly at one another, from our advantage position in the choir stalls. New choirboys were always initiated by being pushed and pulled through a holly bush hedge on the Sylvan Road side of the church. I notice that this holly bush hedge is no longer there, looking at google earth today. I was picked to sing at St Paul's Cathedral in London with many other choirboys from all over London for a special occasion. On another occasion the choir recorded a record of our singing in the church. My father was the church treasurer and a sidesman for many years. Father was confirmed after me, I can still remember him and the others to be confirmed that day filing past me in the Vestry whilst I was dressed in choir boys' cassock and surplice waiting to process into the church for the service of confirmation by the bishop. The only payment I received was when we were asked to sing at weddings. Or once, which was very unusual, we were asked to sing at a funeral. A wedding was 2 shillings (10p) and the funeral was 1 shilling (5p). I did a paper round for about five years, at 7/6d (36p) per week, getting up early very morning except Christmas Day. You may have realised that the church was a very "high church" almost Roman Catholic but aligned to the Church of England, we were known as Anglo Catholics. I understand that it is down to the vicar what he wants high or low church. One of the priests was an elderly man named The Rev. Bardsley. He was related to Dr Cuthbert Bardsley the Archbishop of Coventry Cathedral in those days. At a choir practice one evening the Choir Master and Organist, Mr Betteridge looked at us sopranos and said, "One of you boys is off key. please sing the scale, one boy at a time please". We all sang the scale la,la,la in key. Well, I was the culprit, my voice was breaking. I was taken off the choir pews and had the honour of sitting next to the organised during services, helping where needed, i.e. turning pages and pulling or pushing an organ stop or two etc. I understand that prior to electric organs like the one at St. Johns the old organs were operated by air and had to be pumped by a boy pushing and pulling a lever up and down. That was according to my father. I never moved to be a male member of the choir such as a bass. baritone, tenor, or alto. Just for interest my mother's brother Tom Tunmore was a tenor in the choir at Salisbury Cathedral. This was professional position which he was paid a salary. He had another part time job that of bailiff in the Wiltshire County. In a strange way I was a little upset that my voice was breaking because I enjoyed being a soprano.

I was a newspaper boy for most of my school days. The Newsagents as at 285, South Norwood Hill, SE25 6AP and is now called Crystal Convenience Store. One morning the newsagent said to me, "You've worked many years for us without fault, I will increase your wage from 7 shillings and sixpence to 8 shillings a week". I was so pleased a whole sixpence more. People didn't give tips to paper boys in those days. However, one Christmas Eve morning an old lady opened her door and gave me sixpence, saying "Happy Christmas young man". That was the first and only time I ever saw a person I delivered newspapers to, and my only tip in five or so years. I saved hard and bought a second-hand Raleigh Lenton bicycle with Sturmey-Archer four speed hub gears and hub lighting for £20. I joined the Cyclists Tour Club and went out every weekend with them. On the first occasion it was raining cats and dogs. My mother tried to talk me out of going, but I was going hell or high water. I put an extra coat of shoe polish on my shoes and checked my cycle cape for holes and said goodbye.

I cycled many miles in my youth around South London, Surrey and Kent becoming very fit. I even cycled from home in Upper Norwood right through London south to north then onwards to Forncett End Norfolk about 100 miles, where a second cousin Gerald Smith lived. I was lucky the weather was ideal for cycling, overcast not too hot and dry. The actual route was from South to North London, up the Barnet Bypass. A comfort break at St. Albans for a snack with paternal Grandad and Grandma. Continue up the A1 to Stevenage then Baldock, along A505 to Great Abington, (It's a small world) Here I cycled north on the A11 to Newmarket, Thetford, and on to Attleborough. Here I turned right to Old Buckingham then left to Bunwell and Forncett End. Gerald Smith's father, Uncle Kenny Smith, ran a butchers' shop, which was attached to their house, where I stayed. I helped to make sausages in the shop and kept Uncle Kenny and Aunt Irene amused by my long bike ride experiences. Gerald's Father Kenny, had a brother, Alan Smith who worked at a motor agent in Diss. In those days it was Chitty's, a Ford Motor Agent later Sheffield-Garner. Well, after a few days in Norfolk Uncle Alan who lived in Forncett St. Peters said to me, "You do not have to cycle all the way back home, I'll organise a lift for you to London on a back of a lorry going to centre of London". I was quite adamant that I was going to ride the 100 miles back home. I was only about 15 years old then and no mobile phones, my parents and relations must have been quite anxious. I bet the land lines from Forncett End and Diss to Falkland Park Avenue were red hot.

We had the complete works of W. Shakespeare in leather bound volumes given to us and I must have improved my reading at about this stage in life. The copper plate pictures were wonderful and helped me to distinguish the characters in the plays.

At the age of seventeen I passed a scholarship to attend a full time one years' Junior Engineering Course at Croydon Polytechnic. I had tried a year earlier in 1953 but failed and was advised to stay at Ingram school for another year and try again.

I worked hard at Croydon Polytechnic School Scarbrook Road, adjacent to Surrey Street. We were taught how to operate lathes, milling machines and pillar drills and learned technical drawing, woodwork higher maths, English, etc. I remember in the woodwork lessons we made small occasional tables out of rough pine wood, amongst other small items. I found it really hard to get the table top level with a hand plan and the wood was getting thinner and thinner. One lunch break I noticed an Undertakers premises near the college. The big doors were open and inside men were making coffins. I asked an employee if I could look at their woodworking machinery. There was a huge planner for planning the coffin lids etc. Being a bit foreword, I told the woodworkers my problem of hand planning a table top level at the technical college across the street. "No problem", they said, "When the woodwork master is not looking bring your table top in here, and we will run it through our planner". I got top marks for having a perfectly smooth level table top. One of the lads on the course was from Caterham, Ted Horton who later joined the same indentured apprenticeship as me at Metal Propellers Limited. We became great friends and still visit each other now.

At this time, my mother had her last chance to organise a holiday for me. That being the period between leaving the Croydon Technical College in July and commencing my apprenticeship. This time it was a fortnight picking plums arranged by Concordia volunteering in the Vale of Evesham. This was an experience for me to meet other teenagers from UK and some other European countries, Germany being one. The German boys turned out to be great fun, nobody mentioned the war, except once when one posh English boy in the plum orchard shouted out, "The great RAF", as a flight of fighter planes flew overhead.

This is part of my Grandfathers Indenture followed by mine. It is uncanny with similarities of these documents considering the time lapse 60 years 2 months. I cannot recollect why my Indentures were signed a year after I commenced the apprenticeship. The only reason being would be a convenient time when all three parties were at Croydon or after a probation period at East Cowes, Isle of Wight.

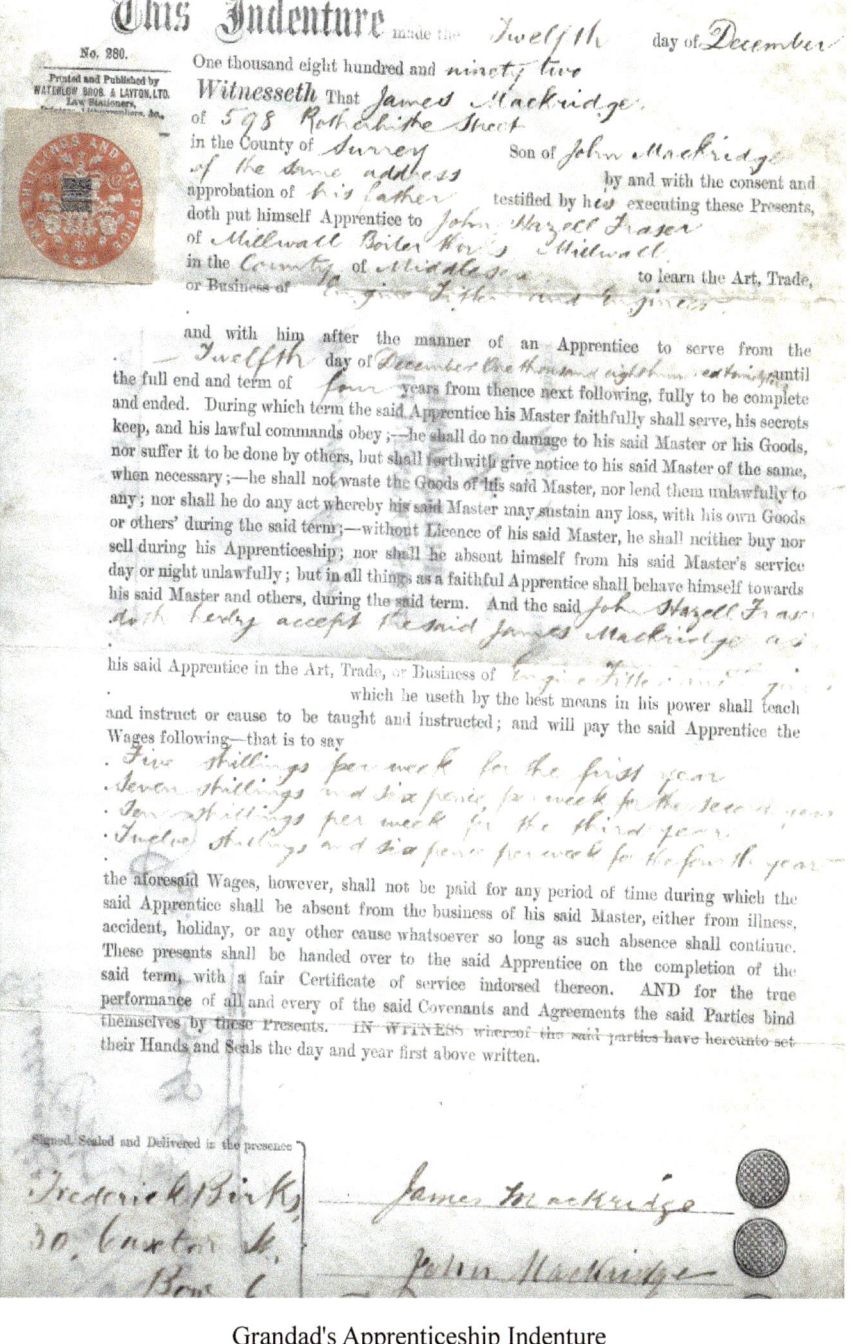

Grandad's Apprenticeship Indenture

I have always treasured my Indentures and very proud when asked for them to give proof of my status.

I do not know if this system of indentures still exits in industry. I have heard of something called Btecs but I'm not sure.

Traditionally an Indenture was signed by the three parties then torn in half, one half given to the apprentice and the other kept by the employer. On completion of the successful apprenticeship the employer gave his half to the apprentice. The apprentice now applying for employment could show that he was fully skilled by displaying the two halves neatly matched along the tear in the document.

I was given one day a week release to attend a local Technical College. I studied for the City & Guilds Certificate in Sheet Metal Work, containing the intermediate and advanced degrees, I obtained first class and intermediate stages respectively.

I have always shown my complete indentures to a respective employer. I am sure they did not understand this antiquated system of proof of training.

This Indenture made the SEVENTEENTH day of OCTOBER one thousand nine hundred and FIFTY FIVE

BETWEEN Eldon James MACKRIDGE of 35 Falkland Park Avenue, South Norwood, London, S.E. 25 (hereinafter called "the Apprentice") a minor of sixteen years of age on the eighth day of September one thousand nine hundred and fifty-three of the first part and James Frederick MACKRIDGE of 35 Falkland Park Avenue, South Norwood, London S.E. 25 being the father of the Apprentice (hereinafter called "the Guardian") of the second part and METAL PROPELLERS LIMITED whose registered office is situated at 47, Parliament Street, in the County of London, Stainless Steel Specialists (hereinafter called "the Employers") of the third part.

WITNESSETH and it is hereby declared and agreed as follows:—

(1) The Apprentice of his own free will and with the consent of the Guardian hereby binds himself Apprentice to the Employers to learn the trade or craft of Sheet Metal Worker and to serve after the manner of an Apprentice from the thirtieth day of August one thousand nine hundred and fifty-four for a term of 5 years.

(2) The Apprentice and Guardian hereby jointly and severally agree with the Employers as follows:—

of service.

IN WITNESS whereof the said parties to these presents have hereunto set their hands and seals the day and year first before written.

Signed sealed and delivered by the said ELDON JAMES MACKRIDGE in the presence of
Signature of Witness ....
Address ....
Occupation ....

Signed sealed and delivered by the said JAMES FREDERICK MACKRIDGE in the presence of
Signature of Witness ....
Address ....
Occupation ....

Signed sealed and delivered by EDWARD OWEN KNAPMAN for and on behalf of METAL PROPELLERS LIMITED in the presence of
Signature of Witness ....
Address ....

My Apprenticeship Indenture

In September 1954, I successfully passed an entrance exam to be an Indentured Apprentice at Metal Propellers Limited, who were stainless steel specialists, for a five-year period. They did not make propellers, but had in the past made metal propellers for ventilation shafts in the mines. The first year of this indentured apprenticeship was spent at East Cowes Isle of Wight at the Saunders Roe, (who were well known for manufacturing flying boats), Apprentice Training School adjacent to Osborne House. East Cowes.

At East Cowes Isle of Wight, we were housed in dormitories that were formerly accommodation for the Royal Navy cadet college between the wars. In the Second World War it was a Royal Naval hospital. When it was a naval cadet's college it was famous for the "Winslow Boy" story. Set against the strict codes of conduct and manners of the time, "The Winslow Boy" is based on a father's fight to clear his son's name. The boy (Ronnie) is expelled from the Osborne Navel College for supposedly stealing a five shilling (25p) postal order without receiving a fair trial. It was made into a film in 1948. Derek Miskin the assistant apprentice supervisor told us this story of "The Winslow Boy". Being on the Isle of Wight was a great opportunity for me to live away from my family, and have a "rest" from my mother who always seemed to be checking up on what I was doing in life, she meant well, I think. There was a great mix of boys of all ages from different social classes ranging from secondary modern, grammar schools private and public schools from whom I learnt a lot. One little song that has stuck in my mind was: - "Lloyd George knew my father, Father knew Lloyd George", which was sang over and over. This being one of many school boy songs. The Training School and dormitories were contained in an area where there were experimental ditching tanks, for the testing of model sea plane hulls for research and to ascertain a perfect shape. It was great fun to hide some unfriendly apprentice's bicycle under the surface of the water. It later came apparent that copper sulphite had been placed in the water to stop underwater plant growth and the bicycles when found where in a copper plated state. The training instructors were made up by three main instructors, "Pop", Vic Stevenson the supervisor's father, a small man Fred who we called the gnome due to his height, and in the drawing office, "Pup" Saunders, who we thought was related to Saunders-Roe. You can imagine these men were of great age. The ex- public-school boys were fond of playing pranks on everyone and even the instructors.

I was never that brave, in case I was caught out. I formed some great friendships, some whom I still met up with now include Ted Horton who now lives in Sherborne, Dorest and Neville Gay who now lives in France. Ted and I were not really friends until we were at Metal Propellers. It was too expensive to return home every weekend, so we either studied or cycled via the chain ferry to West Cowes to see the yachting community and their boats. The biggest annual event was "Cowes Week" a Regatta in mid-August. The world and his wife came to Cowes to see the latest yachts and the celebrities, it was very entertaining to walk round the town looking at all the sights and posh ladies. We sometimes hired a rowing boat, splitting the cost between us, to row under all the landing piers to get an even closer view. Think about it. There was an Isle of Wight car rally each year that was formed in the late 1940's. One of the older apprentices from the accommodation entered a brand-new car, a Vauxhall Velox the year I was there, it was financed by his family. The rally started on the main land, and it was very interesting to see the rally cars coming off the ferry in West Cowes. One weekend, some bright spark announced he would like to cycle around the island and was anyone interested in joining him. I was up for this idea, and eventually six others joined in. We estimated it was about 70 miles in total. We kept to main roads and set off for Newport, the capital, then west to Yarmouth, the Needles down the military road to Chale and St, Catherine's point, the most southerly point of the Isle of Wight. We were all really tired so decided to call for a halt and rest. Most of us were for returning by going north to Newport then back to East Cowes. It was a pity we didn't achieve our objective. I might have completed the circular route around the island if I was alone. I was not so fit since living at East Cowes. I had easily ridden 100 miles a day from London to Norfolk and back, a few years early. Cowes was two areas, East Cowes and West Cowes with the month of the river Medina being the line dividing them. A chain ferry was the only way to travel between East and West, and I guess it was well used by us. There was, (or still is) a HM Prison at Parkhurst just north of Newport near the centre of the island. When a prisoner escaped news quickly informed all inhabitants on the island to be on their guard and make sure all light sea craft were made secure. Living on the Isle of Wight we were near all things naval and aircraft. One day out on my cycle at Whippingham two naval aircraft passed low overhead a Fairey Gannet and a Westland Wyvern both had turboprop contra-rotating propellers, I waved at the pilots and one waved back, it made my day.

Whilst I was at Saunders Roe the company had just lost a contract to sell the SR 45 Princess flying boat to BOAC, (British Overseas Airways Corporation). Ideas had changed and the land-based airliners like the de Havilland Comet were in favour (It's a small world I would be working on Comet 4's years later at East African Airways) One Princess was at Cowes on the slipway adjacent to the great hangar and two others were cocooned and beached at Calshot Southampton Water. As apprentices we were shown around the Princess Flying Boat it had two decks and even a winding stair case from the top deck to the lower where there was a cocktail bar. There was another type of aircraft that was not wanted, the SR A/1 a jet powered Fighter flying boat that was designed for WW2 in the far east. Work was in progress on a prototype SR53 interceptor, fighter with a ram jet to give it maximum climb capability. I remember part of the main hanger bring curtained off so eyes could not see the highly secret work of developing this futurist fighter. The money earning part of Saunders Roe, was constructing V Bomber cabins for the Valiant V Bomber. I was shown how in an emergency the cabin roof was ejected via explosive bolts prior to the cabin crew ejected using Martin-Baker Ejection seats. All aircraft fuselages were called hulls to remind you of the histrionic connection with flying boats and seaplanes that were constructed at Saunders-Roe.

The Company was also engaged with Sir Christopher Cockerell the designer of the hovercraft, to develop his idea of transport for commercial use. It was very successful for twenty years or so, with the cross-channel car ferry called "Princess Anne" and swamp land military transport. There still is a hovercraft passenger service between Southsea and Ryde on the Isle Wight.

In the Training School workshops, I was shown how to work metal materials ie filing, cutting, forming and joining. The main metal was duralumin an alloy of aluminium and copper which was used in the manufacture of aircraft due to its lightness and strength. We were given blue prints of aircraft parts to hone our skills. I also attended an engineering course at the Technical College Newport Isle of Wight one day a week. Most of the students were apprentices from Saunders-Roe being the biggest employer by far on the island. There were a few students from the islands ship builders, J.S. White being famous for up rating ex Royal Navy frigates, and motor torpedo boats (MTB) etc.

Stainless steel items made by me at Metal Propellers Ltd.

This year away from home, put me on the road to being an adult, so when I was enlisted years later, I handled the adult life easier.

After this first year away from home, we were sent to work with journeymen, that is skilled men, at Metal Propellers these men were very good and treated us like members of a big family. The first skilled man I was assigned to was Stan Taylor others were Tom Gandy, Joe Connetta and many more like Tom Lloyd and Charlie Rowe. Of course, there was a lot of leg pulling about our first date with young ladies. Metal Propellers mainly designed and fabricated large stainless steel cracking towers for the oil industry and stainless-steel equipment for the dairy and food industry. It was heavy noisy work and sometimes not very interesting. A cracking tower consisted of heating crude oil that gradually rose up the tower from floor to floor by travelling up risers arranged over each floor. On the top of the risers were fixed bubble caps to force the oil down and therefore slowing the cracking action down. Heavy oils are extracted near the bottom and higher up the lighter fuels like petrol and aviation fuels. On many occasions the Foreman (Mr Higgins commonly known as Higgy) asked me to make small stainless-steel implements for him personally and the Managers like toast racks, cocktail shakers, and even complete tea services, etc. I was taught metal working practice in mild and stainless steel including free-hand development, wheeling and raising, wiring, beading edges, swaging, and jennying in the manufacture of products. The working day was 9 hours (8 am to 6 pm) with 1 hour for lunch each day. We were also expected to work on Saturday mornings. making 50 hours in total. However, we had one day off each week to attend Technical College at Carshalton Technical College then later at Wimbledon Technical College. I was studying City & Guilds Sheet Metal Work which I obtained first class at intermediate and second class at the advanced stages. My memories of time spent at Metal Propellers seemed rather dull. It was due to this concern that I was troubled to where was this apprenticeship taking me to in later life. I did not like the continual grind each day, clocking in clocking out, the same boring life. I wanted to get out and meet life outside the factory gates. However, military life sorted all that out, and made me stand up straight, be proud and look people in their eyes.

    I had a wonderful life at weekends whilst an apprentice, going to parties meeting young ladies.

Mum & Dad 1954

When I was seventeen, I started to learn to drive in my father's car. a 1953 sit up and beg Ford 8 Anglia. I have included a picture of this car taken at Uncle Alan Smith's house in 1954. My father brought this car new from Uncle Alan's employer Chitty in Diss. After a few months I applied to take my test for a full drivers' license, I failed due to my inexperience. I carried on with my father seating next to me for another month and applied again and passed with flying colours.

I bought a 1932 Austin Seven from a man at work for £12 10 shillings. I was not happy with it and decided to cut the bodywork off the chassis and make an Austin Seven Special in our back garden. When I'd removed the body, the problem was to dispose of it. I cut the body into bits with a hacksaw and dumped them into the dustbin over a matter of weeks. I removed the engine and tuned it with parts that were easily available from specialist manufactures. In those days, cars were expensive due to a very high purchase tax and availability because of the export drive after the war.

The Austin Seven Special was near completion; I became eager to get on the road so I sold it to purchase a 1949 MG TC. Costing £350. I had great fun with this car and kept it until I went abroad with the army.

As I was still on the small size and very gullible everyone thought a great stainless-steel tank would be too much for me to handle, and

National Service would be out of the question due to my physical stature, so I had no hope.

National Service was still active but I was deferred until my apprenticeship was completed at the age of 22 in 1959. On the very month in September 1959, I was called to attend a medical examination for National Service. To the surprise of everyone at work and home I passed A1 fit. Before I was formally posted to the Services I volunteered to enlist as a Craftsman in the Royal Electrical and Mechanical Engineers as a Metal Smith and signed on for 6 years with the Colours as a Regular. I remember a sheet metal worker saying to me, "You are very gullible, Eldon, we all hope you get on alright in the army". I had always wanted to join the Army or Navy but being an Indentured Apprentice I could not break my 'oath'. But in hindsight it was best to complete my training and to become a skilled craftsman and a man. During this period, I was beginning to understand life.

Serving the Queen

8 Flight Army Air Corps training in Tsavo Game Reserve

I was enlisted on 2nd September 1959, (into uniform for the third time, including cubs and choirboy). Basic training was six weeks, at the REME Training barracks Blandford Forum, this included Marching, drill, firing Le Enfield .303 rifles, SLR rifles, Bren guns, light sub machine gun and throwing mills bombs (hand grenades). The first day was a little daunting. I was given my kit and taken to a bed place in a billet and told to wait until there was enough personal to make up a platoon before start training. A Lance Corporal came into the billet and said to a new soldier next to me, "How long have you been in the Army". This man was so proud that he'd been in the room before anyone else, stood up smartly to attention, and said, "All day sir", like an old sweat. This really tickled me and has been a joke with my children and grandchildren. When we go over to see the grandchildren, I say," How long have you been in the army". They stand to attention and say "All day sir", Grandad. During basic training we were told to pay close attention to the firing of fire arms because after the first six weeks' basic soldier training as we could be posted to Cyprus or other countries where there was unrest. After basic training I was granted a one weeks leave and then was posted to Ashchurch in Gloucestershire where there is a very large army vehicle depot. There were literally thousands of vehicles in large hangars motorbikes, Land Rovers, Bedford 3 toners, Commers, Austin, Morris, Humber's and Scammells, armoured cars and tanks etc. As a skilled craftsman I worked on Austin Ambulances a lot, like the ones used in the Second World War. In fact, very similar to the Ambulance in the film "Ice Cold in Alex" about a war story in the desert starring John Mills. "It's a small world".

I worked as a sheet metal worker/welder on all types of ground warfare wheeled vehicles. To get promotion I needed First Class Trade, First Class Education, and First-Class Military Cadre. I had education and trade due to my apprenticeship, so I was sent to Warminster Garrison on a Cadre Course to gain First Class Military which was successful. As soon as I arrived back at Ashchurch I was posted again this time to Middle Wallop the Army Air Corps Centre to be evaluated as an Air Frames technician (Sheet Metal Worker and Welder). The Army records department assumed that as I served my apprenticeship with a company called Metal Propellers Limited, I was an aircraft technician. I was then sent to RAF Weeton near Kirkham, Lancashire on an Air Frames Course. This was a RAF training camp for drivers and included training of many trades and skills for not only men but personnel of the WRAF. It seemed strange to eat meals with young ladies in the mess. This was the furthest I had travelled from home and it seemed a little strange, even the railway carriages were a different colour.

One weekend I went to Blackpool with some other lads on the course. The Blackpool Tower was breath taking and being so far from home it was all very exciting at the time. Little did I know that this was nothing to which I was about to experience in a few weeks' time. I passed the course with flying colours. Being a first-class Craftsman on the course I was up for a posting of my choice. I was given a choice of Northern Ireland, Cyprus, Germany or North Africa. I took North Africa with the Army Air Corps. It was 8 Independent Reconnaissance Flight, Army Air Corps which was due to move to Kenya in East Africa from Tripoli Libya. I then waited for a boring month at the REME Depot in Poperinge Barracks Arborfield Garrison for a flight to Tripoli. The only interesting occasions was listening to the stories of soldiers returning from far away postings. On one occasion there was a problem in my barrack hut concerning our procedure and I was elected to report this to the officer in charge. When I asked my colleagues why they had chosen me, they stated that as I was the only southerner and they were northerners I would be understood. This proved to me I had a southern accent. My Mother told me a cousin of my fathers was teaching near Nairobi. And another relation lived in South Africa, maybe I could visit them. Winnie Foy in Nairobi was a possibility but South Africa was out of the question. My Mum had no idea of the size of the Continent of Africa and the distance from East Africa to South Africa.

Eventually I was transported to an air field in Stansted, Essex. I had never flown before. The aircraft was a Bristol Britannia with the seats facing backwards and a lot of crying children. The flight was what the army called a "trooper flight", lots of married soldiers, wives, and their families.

We took off, and after a short time the pilot announced that there was a little problem and we had to return to Stansted, after dumping all the fuel in the wing tanks. Oh dear, and my first flight.

However, when we had been in the transit hall for an hour, we set off again. With many hours in the air after this incident, I never experienced such a problem whilst flying, civilian or military.

We landed at Idris Airport, Tripoli, Libya at about midnight on 21st June 1960. As I was travelling unattached, rather than with a group, an Arab took me to a bedroom not far from the airport. In the morning I found a mess for breakfast and a waiter came to take my order. This all seemed different. In England, all the soldiers had to queue for food at meal times. After breakfast, I found my way to the hangar where 8 Flight was located. A Royal Navy Chief Petty Officer greeted me asking if I had found the other ranks accommodation last night. The Army Air Corps in 1960 were short of technicians so it was made up of Royal Artillery, REME, RAF and Fleet Air Arm personnel. The CPO asked me where I'd got to last night, I couldn't be found. When I told him, he laughed out loud? I had slept in the Officers' Mess. This CPO O'Flaherty was to became a great friend of mine in East Africa. He helped me with airframe repairs especially on the Auster Mark 9 fuselage and aileron which were fabric covered. He had great experience of working on the Royal Navy aircraft carrier-based Fairy Swordfish biplane bomber that was used in the second world war with great success although it was obsolescent then and retired in 1945.

I found myself at RAF Castel Benito where my unit was and then taken to the OR (other ranks) accommodation, the whole place had been built by Mussolini to resemble Roman architecture and looked really grand.

Here is a short history, "8 Flight can trace history to the Royal Air Force No. 1908 Air Observation Post Flight formed on 31st December 1946, disbanded on 7th October 1955 and later reformed on 16th October that year.

On 1st September 1957, 8 Flight Army Air Corps was formed as 8th Reconnaissance Flight Army Air Corps with the transfer of AOP Flight based at RAF Idris in Libya to the newly formed Army Air Corps. The Flight relocated to Kenya where it was re-designated as 8 Flight AAC. The Flight subsequently relocated to Aden for the troubles there. Then to Northern Ireland, then on to the Falklands War. In the late 1990s to AAC Netheravon Salisbury Plain. In 2000 the flight relocated to Stirling Lines Credenhill Herefordshire. In 2001 the flight was incorporated into the Joint Forces Aviation Wing. In 2008 to SAS (Special Air Service). On the 1st September 2013, 8 Flight AAC was re-designated as 658 Squadron AAC. In June 2017 the Squadron landed a helicopter on London Bridge to provide support to the Metropolitan Police Service in response to the London Bridge terrorist attack".

During June it was very hot as I have mentioned, we worked during the first part of the day and laid on our beds in the afternoon mainly listening to Radio Wheelus from a local US Air Force Base or playing chess etc. Some just slept (called Egyptian PT or blanket pressing). On a day off, I managed to go to Tripoli, and walk down 24th of December Street and visit the bar that featured in the film, "Ice Cold in Alex". Happy Days.

The Army Air Corps was formed with the amalgamation of the Glider Pilot Regiment and the then Royal Air Force AOP (Air Observation Posts). The AOP were used to report gun fire accuracy for the Royal Artillery. The compliment were pilot officers and N.C.O's from many regiments, Royal Artillery, Royal Electrical and Mechanical Engineers, Fleet Air Arm, Royal Air Force and other supporting personnel staff such as Royal Army Ordnance Corps and Royal Medical Corps, etc.

The summer weather in Tripoli was hot, as you would expect, very hot, dry and not a cloud in sight. One afternoon after work I noticed the sun disappearing and it grew quite dark. I said to a fellow squaddie, "Looks like rain is coming", he replied, "You'll be lucky, it's a Ghibli". A Ghibli is a word for a strong south easterly wind that picks up the fine sand from the desert and covers everything and the barrack floors in sand. Another name is a sirocco, I believe. At break times Arabs and Italians from the N.A.A.F.I. delivered food to our hangar, i.e. milk frozen in cartons, cheese and onion rolls etc. I had never eaten raw white onions before and got a taste for it. "Mukka" is the Arabic word for friend so we were always called mukka, johnnie or tommie. It always amazed me when on manoeuvres in the desert miles from anywhere, how an Arab would appear from nowhere and try to sell an egg to you when you hadn't seen a living sole let alone a chicken for days.

Out in the desert one day we came across a lone Land Rover moving very slowly with, as it transpired, two National Servicemen. We asked them if they needed any help. "No, we are conducting an experiment to ascertain how far one can drive, in this heat without oil and water in the engine of a Land Rover". "How far have you driven", we said. The reply was "N miles". I was amazed what a Land Rover engine could stand such punishment and how two soldiers could destroy MOD property, and wondered if they were ever caught and put on a fizzer. The Flight had one D.H. Chipmunk aircraft for training purposes and a plaything for pilot officers. I managed to get a flight one-day seating in the rear of the twin cockpit. Great fun, flying over the desert dunes very low one moment then up high up in the sky upside down almost hanging from your seat straps. After getting use to the desert and heat I enjoyed my time in Tripoli. The Crown Prince Iris was still running the country, before General Gadiffi came to power.

The desert although hot and deserted had a magical feeling. The main thing was not to think you were lost but go with the flow. I also had an opportunity to visit one or two other British army bases in Libya.

Me on Leave 1961

Kenya

After two months, the Flight moved to Kenya in August 1959. I was not in possession of a British Passport; one was issued to me by the British Consul in Tripoli stating that I was a "Government Employee" so I was able to travel by air to East Africa. How I managed to get to Tripoli in Libya without a passport has always amazed me. I travelled by air with the advance party, the rest travelled in a large landing ship to Mombasa and then by road to the Nairobi Garrison, where I was to stay for the next four years.

After disembarking from the aircraft, we travelled by lorry and arrived on 23rd August 1960 at Nairobi Garrison which was situated on Langata Road, opposite the airfield (which was an old RNAS Royal Naval Air Service airfield from the First World War) about 4 miles north west of Nairobi. I was amazed that the sky was full of white clouds, not like Libya with a complete blue sky, wall to wall. Our hangar was situated amongst private light aircraft companies. and the Kenya Police Air Wing hangars. The 8th Independent Reconnaissance Flight, Army Air Corps occupied half a large hangar. The total number of aeroplanes was six Auster Mark 9's. After time these were replaced by de Havilland Beavers and Sud Aviation Allouette helicopters. 8 Flight being attached to the 24 Infantry Brigade we were available to deal with any disturbance which may arise in East Africa or even Radfan mountains in Aden.

We were needed on flood and famine relief and aid the civil power in Zanzibar, census operations also Kenya in the remote country inhabited by the Masai Tribe, and helping Kenya in ceremonial events for the "Uhuru" Freedom.

I was the only metal worker/welder and due to fire precautions, I worked outside in a shelter constructed from an Auster aircraft packing box. One of my other main duties was driving a Bedford RL type Light Recovery Lorry. I was known as "Weldon the Eldon" by the flight technical personnel as I was the lone welder and airframe engineer and very important.

I had many exciting times with the Recovery Lorry, when the Flight was on manoeuvres, I was tail end Charlie in case a vehicle broke down, I would then tow it until a Vehicle Mechanic could repair it or was deemed unfit for local service and taken to REME workshops at Kahawa, so named after coffee. The storey goes that when the Army were looking for an area to build the 24th Infantry Brigade Headquarters in Kenya by looking at maps it was noticed that the word "kahawa" covered the suitable area. When asked what the word "kahawa" meant in English, "coffee fields". was the reply. So, it was agreed to name the army base Kahawa, situated about 10 miles from Nairobi.

One day we were driving through the bush, miles from anywhere, when the vehicle in front of me, a Commer instrument repair box lorry, stopped. The driver, Cpl Peter Grayston, jumped out of his cab and shouted to me "I've slowed down to let the convoy disappear, do you want a holiday?" His plan was for me to follow him off the trail and get lost in the bush on purpose. We had plenty of fuel, food and water to last and have some freedom for a few days. After many miles it started to rain heavily, and it could really rain in Kenya. I came aware that it was not just the rain making the noise but a helicopter hovering low over ahead. The pilot was trying to communicate with me for landing signals.
 I landed him with recognisable hand signals. The pilot officer thanked me saying how pleased he was with himself for finding us and gave us instructions how to re-join the convoy who had stopped to make camp for the night. The whole thing was thought to be a genuine mistake. At least we had given the pilot some practice at "seek and find".
 Travelling in convoy had its surprises. One late afternoon, we came to a crossing barge at a river-crossing operated by tribesmen pulling on ropes. The river was flowing quite fast, and the only means to cross was by a barge pulled slowly by a group of tribesmen pulling on a rope fixed at both sides of the river. Our convoy was made up of over ten Land Rovers and 3 ton Bedford Lorries, and me in the Recovery Truck etc. and there was a few civilian lorries and cars. Each crossing was taking over 10 minutes. It would be dark before we had all got across. I manoeuvred my recovery lorry to the front of the line of vehicles and asked if I could be pulled across as I had an idea. Most British Army lorries have a winch fitted which can pull from either the front or rear. via a drum of rope wire fixed horizontal under the chassis. When I was across the river, I asked the Africans to attach my winch cable to their barge and pull the cable back to the opposite river bank. Now on the other side, the barge

was attached to the winch of another Army lorry. Our two lorries then pulled the barge backwards and forwards across the river transporting the whole convoy, and civilians in quick time with a huge bow wave to the great amusement of the African ferry operators as they were able to take a break and laugh at Tommie's great idea, "Mzuri sana".

On another occasion I was making good process to catch up with the convoy when a rhinoceros came out of the savannah just ahead on the right-hand side. I changed down a gear and gunned the petrol engine. The rhino put his head down and offered his horn up to my right front tyre. Stories that I had heard of rhinos turning vehicles over came in to my head. I began to accelerate but my attacker matched my speed. It seemed I was in great trouble here. But at last, the animal veered off away off the track back into the savannah. I still have nightmares regarding this moment.

One day in a game reserve I was driving a long behind the convoy when I noticed in my rear-view mirror a helicopter travelling behind me at almost ground level and closing on me at a great rate. Just as it was about to hit the rear of my vehicle it gained height and flew over me. I ducked to the floor of the cab in fright as the helicopter roared away. After some days I found out which pilot officer had played this game on me, and we had a polite chuckle. "Full out the officers".

Me Exercising Rhino

I always volunteered for anything going to give me a spice of life. I was asked by the Commanding Officer one day if I would take my recovery truck to Nairobi Game Reserve Wardens area where the Vets had a rhinoceros in a stockade in a bad way. The rhino had some illness that had stopped the blood in its front legs (pins and needles). The handlers had ropes under and around the animal. The idea was for me to lift and lower the rhino until the pins and needles were cured. In other words, physiotherapy on a large scale

The Army Reporters and Photographer were in attendances and the whole thing went viral, I had my picture in the Daily Express with the recovery truck and that poor rhino.

In June/July 1962 a team of soldiers from the Flight were organising a walk to the top of Kilimanjaro and wanted volunteers, I thought this was a good idea.

We had lots of practice climbs on smaller hills and mountains locally. The team consisted of one officer and about six OR's. (other ranks).

Kilimanjaro is 19,340 feet above sea level, however, we had good start due to the fact that we were living at about 1.800 feet at Nairobi Garrison. The ascent took us about three days. We slept in a tin hut the night before the final ascent just below the snow cap.

I notice these days due to global warming the snow cap has receded or even disappeared in places.

Me dressed in clothes suitable to conditions at different altitudes on Mount Kilimanjaro

On the mountain, we met some sailors from a ship docked in Mombasa, they were in a bad way due to a great altitude change. Near the top, on the snow cap, the only thing that I wanted was a bowel movement. 2nd Lt. Alan Blaxall told me to go to the edge of a glacier, relieve myself and try to make good covering it with my ice pick with snow. It may still be there, but due to global warming, watch out!!

The return trip to the Outward-Bound Hut, Base Camp took us half a day.

It is a requirement of the British Army that personnel are always clean shaven (except a Pioneer Corps. Sergeant who always have a full beard). While on the mountain, above a certain altitude, we had special permission that allowed us to be unshaven.

After a night's rest and a shave at an Outward-Bound base camp we returned to Nairobi Garrison via Land Rover.

Kenya gained independence on the 12th December 1963. Many months before Independence Day (Uhuru in Swahili) we witnessed sealed army trucks arriving at Nairobi Garrison for a night stop en route to Mombasa Docks from army barracks up north. I was told that they were carrying very sensitive war material that had to be taken out of Kenya before Uhuru. We were ordered to remain in the Garrison Barracks that day. All went smoothly until the 24th January 1964 when the Kenyan Army (Formerly The Kings African Rifles) mutinied over their dissatisfaction of low pay. The new Kenyan government requested help from the British Government. Most of the strength of 24 Infantry Brigade in Kenya were deployed in Aden. So before re-enforcements could arrive all non-combatant soldiers, in other words' not the infantry, guards, Royal Marines, artillery or S.A.S were ordered to protect important areas such as the radio station, telephone exchange, overseas cable office important government buildings, and Embakasi Airport. I was with a contingent ordered to protect the National Airport at Embakasi. We were loaded on to 3-ton army lorries dressed in full battle order dress and armed to the teeth. I was a Bren gunner and as we jumped off the lorry an officer shouted, "Look smart men, show them we mean business". I had a Bren gun and many rounds of ammunition in my ammo pouches and webbing, and no way was I going to jump 4 to 5 feet to the ground and break my legs. A member of our crew took my gun and said, "Jump Mac". I hit the ground and tried to maintain my smart British stiff upper lip. We patrolled the Airport until we were relieved by a section of Royal Horse Artillery from Nakuru, up country.

The Aircraft Carrier, HMS Centaur had left Portsmouth on the 24th January 1964 on route to Aden and was diverted to Mombasa via Dar-es-Salaam with 45 Commando Royal Marines to help if trouble broke out.

All three East African counties armies Kenya, Uganda, and Tanganyika were involved in mutiny regarding low pay and slow promotion. I think that some 350 members of the Uganda Rifles based at Jinja near Lake Victoria had detained their British officers and Uganda's Minister of Home Affairs. After a few days the local governments worked a settlement out to solve the problem and things went back to normal. I can understand how the African soldier felt when he compared the British soldiers rate of pay to his pay.

HMS CENTAUR

HMS CENTAUR on 24 January 1964. In that month there was a mutiny by the Army in Tanganyika. Britain was asked to help but no Commando Carrier was available, thus CENTAUR displayed the inherent flexibility of carrier aviation by proceeding to Aden to pick up 45 Commando Royal Marines, 16/5 Lancers and two RAF BELVEDERE helicopters. She carried all these at high speed to Dar-es-Salaam together with her own air group. Landrovers and Ferret armoured cars can be seen to starboard forward of Fly 1. It remained possible to operate the SEA VIXENS but it would have been a squeeze! Once off Tanganyika, the military force was landed by the anti-submarine WESSEX helicopters of 815 Squadron and CENTAUR stood off with her fighters and GANNETS ready, if necessary, to support the force ashore.

In April, 1964 HMS Centaur was still in the Indian Ocean off the East African coast and the Army Air Corps wanted to prove that they could liaise with the Navy by delivering goods or personnel on to aircraft carriers if needed in an emergency. A volunteer was wanted to be an observer with the pilot of a de Havilland Beaver on practising deck landings and take off procedure on HMS Centaur. A Beaver was not fitted with any form of deck arrester equipment. The exercise was to see if a Beaver could accomplish aircraft carrier deck landings during the Aden war. The Beaver had very good STOL capabilities so it was estimated that it was possible.

I was not a good swimmer. There wasn't anyone interested. So here I went again. I had a quick word with the pilot who told me not to worry, the Navy have all the equipment if we go in the drink. A helicopter is always flying beside the carrier when aircraft are landing or taking off the deck and will recover anyone who is in the sea. That's a relieve.

    We flew to Mombasa Airport to refuel. We then set off east over the Indian Ocean. The Pilot said if we go in the drink, pull the lever to jettison the door first, then pull the cord to inflate your life jacket, otherwise you will not get out due to the small door with a large inflated life jacket. We couldn't see any aircraft carrier in sight, then he shouted over the intercom, "Look at that tiny grey thing". Flying over sea you have no perception of height. We flew over the deck which was rising and lowering about six feet, *nice and calm for you* came a voice in my ears from HMS Centaur control tower. That said, we went for it, me with hands on the lever and cord. Nearer and nearer the deck came towards us, and bump, bump, brakes on, stop. I was not too sure what was to happen next, but I was alive. I jumped out and ran across to the control island while the sailors pushed the Beaver back for a take-off. I was welcomed by an Artillery Officer who was pleased to see me, being a fellow soldier. We watched while the Beaver accomplished two more landings and take-offs, then flew off without me. The Army officer handed me over to a Fleet Air Arm Sailor. There was a call over the loud speakers, action stations, action stations. I was led across to the edge of the flight deck to an anti-aircraft gun. The team were ready to fire on command from an officer. An anti-flash mask was hastily place on my head. "Practice fire at will, FIRE" came the order. The noise was deafening, I thought a flash mask was all very well, but I could do with ear plugs. At last, the order came "Cease firing", the gunners took no notice but carried on firing. "Cease firing" again the second time the order was disobeyed. Stop firing those f......guns. At last silence. I asked what was that all about. Well, I was informed, the gunners knowing it was practice firing continued firing until the whole clip of heavy shells were fired so they did not have the hard work of unloading a half-used clip of shells. The gun was cleared safe, all the shells fired and the gun declared unloaded.

    I spent a night on board and after breakfast was flown back to Mombasa Airport by a Westland Whirlwind helicopter, which was on a Services Mail trip. I then was flown by Beaver back to Nairobi. I cannot remember anyone asking where I had been, it seemed as long as I was in one piece all was OK, good fun all-round for me. Also, I had one day of my service career in the Royal Navy adding to the three weeks at RAF Weedon (Blackpool) on a training course I saw service in all three Services, except the Royal Marines.

On Film set for "Dr Moses"

The film stars Robert Mitcham and Carroll Baker plus others and a film crew were in Kenya about 1964/5 shooting the film 'Doctor Moses'. One scene depicts a helicopter crashing and being burnt out by local tribesmen. One of our Allouette helicopters was used and the Film Directors asked if we could make a mock-up of the helicopter on fire. You can't use a real helicopter. Two Sergeant's, Bob Driscoll & Brian Balham, Cpl Roger Poll and myself formed a business company to manufacture a mock up Allouttee helicopter. We managed to acquire some real parts from the stores that were not wanted and we manufactured the rest. On completion we delivered the mock helicopter to the film company on the film set in the bush. When the film was released, I went to see it. For all our trouble it was only on the screen a matter of seconds. It just shows you what lengths film makers go to in filming a story.

There had been abnormal rainfalls and floods in East Africa during 1961 while I was serving there. The Army and RAF had helped the local inhabitants during this unfortunate time. The British Government showed their respects to the forces by sending the Secretary of State for War John Profumo CBE, and his wife Valerie

Hobbs an actress to thank us. I was selected to attend Governors House, and as we filed in we were ordered by Malcolm MacDonald the Governor to throw our headgear into a heap of navy blue and RAF hats in the entrance. I was glad our berets were pale blue and easy to find after the reception. We were introduced to John Profumo and Valerie Hobbs who shook our hands thanking us individually. We asked John Profumo when the National Service would end, he stated that the last call up was on December 31st 1960 and the finish would be in April 1963. Little did we know that at this time John Profumo had been in the company of Christine Keeler the 21 years of age show girl and Mandy Rice-Davis since 1961. On the 23rd March 1963 John Profumo quit his position in the Government. The newspapers reported that Christine Keeler attended Court on the 22nd July 1963. Christine Keller died in 2017 after a much troubled life.

Living in Kenya and working with the nationals I soon began to speak a little up-country Swahili. This language is made up from many other languages like Arabic, French, native tribal and simple English, but of course, writing in Swahili is a little more difficult. I still speak a little Swahili and taught my children and grandchildren to talk a few Swahili words and phrases for fun. I was in a London departmental store once and over heard two men discussing the cost of a pullover in Swahili. I put my two-penny worth of Swahili into their chat, well, they were really surprised they said to me they didn't expect to hear a white man in London speaking Swahili. The same happen years later at a Haverhill carnival with a Masai dance group that jumped very high. I greeted them in Swahili, "Jambo habari gani" they replied, "Mzuri sana Bwana". They were really pleased to greet an Englishman speaking Swahili in the depths of Suffolk.

Life with 8 Flight was really good fun, the corps de spirit was great. Some described it as a private flying club. The night life in the bars and night clubs was great with good food and company.

When we were dressed in khaki drill number three uniform pressed by the African laundry men, for a parade, the sailors called us cardboard soldiers. The Africans ironing of khaki drill uniforms is something not to be missed. An iron heated by charcoal was used. Then with a bowl of starch and water the African took a large mouthful of starch and blew it out over the Khaki drill in a fine spray from his mouth then quickly ironed the material so it was stiff on drying. Not recommend for ironing in the UK.

My sister, Heather married while I was in the Army abroad and I made a surprise visit to England for her Wedding. I dressed in number one dress i.e. dark blue uniform with gold thread badges, and a red strip down each trouser leg, much to my mother's delight.

A cousin of my father, Winnie Foy, was a teacher at Limuru Girls School a few miles north of Nairobi. I saw her on many occasions and even stayed in one of the dormitories during the school holidays. Limuru was a very pleasant place being at higher altitude than Nairobi, a light frost after sunset was a great relief from the equator sunshine.

Farmers up country occasional advertised for servicemen in East Africa to stay on farms for a holiday. I applied with another soldier called Norman for a fortnight at Cottam Farm near Kitale. The Army provided transport to and from the location. Mr Crompton and his wife Jill farmed a large farm with sheep, cows, ducks and chickens and coffee. The farm was not at the right altitude tea crops, but it was good for livestock and the coffee. The farmhouse was all on one level and was built by the farmer after the First World War. Their children were all grown up and had left. We were accommodated in the farmhouse. There were several Africans servants in the house under the charge of an African butler. The food was first class. One morning the Mr Crompton asked me to go with an African farmworker in a Morris Minor pickup to select a suitable sheep for dinner. When a sheep had been selected the farmworker jumped out of the vehicle, knife at the ready, grabbed the animal, slit its throat and hung it by the rear legs to a convenient acacia tree for the blood to gush out on to the ground. I had never seen anything like this before. No licensed abattoir here, just a licence to kill. We had mutton for dinner that evening. Beautiful, however, I put the slaughter to the back of my mind. Jill Crompton wrote a letter to my mum in a mother-to-mother sort of way, to say how I was, and in safe hands: -

"Cottam Farm
P.O. Box 470
Kitale
Kenya
14th June 1961

Dear Mrs Mackridge,

We have just had Eldon and a friend staying with us for a fortnight. I thought you might like to have a letter from me about their visit. Eldon is very well & happy! Thoroughly enjoys the life out here.
   We were afraid they might find it a bit dull with two oldish people miles from anywhere, but they both seemed to enjoy farm life and were very good at making their own amusements. I said time had gone so quickly that they had not been able to do all the things they wanted to do.
   Eldon says he would like to come again and we shall be very pleased to have him – we really enjoyed their visit.

Yours sincerely,
Jill Crompton."

I enjoyed chatting to Mr Crompton and learning the history of the white Kenyan farmer. The first Land Regulation Act in 1897 did not attract many European farmers, but after the First World War in 1919 many ex-soldiers took up Lord Delamare's offer of one farthing per acre. After the Second World War many more ex- service men became Kenyan farmers and the population of Europeans rose to 23.033 much less than that of South Africa but they had good relations with the local Africans, and the output was wide including maize, coffee, tea, and dairy products for instances. Mr Crompton told us many stories about his exploits in the First World War as an army officer.
   At one meal time an African servant said to me, "Leta Ku chupa nyeusi kidogo". I translated this to "did I want a small black bottle". After sitting there for a short time with my hosts smiling at me and me not wanting to appear silly thought I would say, "Ndiyo" meaning, yes, and see what he would bring. Guess what he brought to the table, a small bottle of MARMITE. Luckily my favourite.
   We spent most days helping around the farm and listening to the

wireless in the evening with the Mr & Mrs Crompton. The farm was too far from civilisation to be connected to the East African Power and Lighting Company so a diesel or petrol generator was in use during the day then at night Mr Crompton switched it off. If we wanted to read late at night a large battery in the circuit would help, but would gradually run down. It was a lovely holiday and it all came to an end after two weeks when the Land Rover arrived to return us to the Nairobi Garrison.

The nationals in service were generally treated very well. I did, however, see some army NCO's and commissioned officers ride roughshod over Africans mainly up country. The media was not present then as now, so during small uprisings that the army had to attend to "things" sometimes went unreported.

On 12th December 1963 Kenya attained independence (Uhuru). from the UK. We thought there may be some sort trouble aimed at us, but things continued in the same happy way.

I was offered a job with East African Airways on de Havilland Comet B4, Dakota, Fokker Friendships and an associated company Seychelles & Kilimanjaro Airways who flew de Havilland Dragonfly Rapids or Dominies deployed on local passenger routes. I left the Army and continued living in East Africa working at Nairobi Embakasi Airport. However, I did work for a small company called Safari Air Services for a few months before starting with East African Airways. I worked on aircraft called Cessna 105 or 172 that are still manufactured today in some form. The Kenyan farmers up country used this type of aircraft to travel from farm to farm and to collect supplies from Nairobi. I had many jobs rebuilding wings, that had been damaged and even travelled into the bush to repair aircraft. It appeared that farmers flew to parties at a neighbours' farm and sometimes crashed after drinking too much sauce. These jobs, sometimes needed an overnight stop at a posh hotel, like the Brooke Bond tea hotel which was one of the best. At first I lived in Nairobi at the Kirk Road House, accommodation ran by the local council for mainly single people. The manager and his wife Sonia, brought or leased a hotel called the "Normandy" in a leafy suburb of Nairobi and asked me if I would like to live at their new hotel. This was rather more up market for about the same cost, so I took up their offer.

This was an interesting time; very good wages, good friends, free flights locally and three free international flights each year. I travelled to London once on this concession. I remember that we had an engine change on a de Havilland Comet 4B at Heathrow once. Being an airframe technician and the engines being in the root of the wing I had to remove and replace a small amount of panelling (skin). I stayed at LHR for two days accommodated at Skyways Hotel on the A4 just adjacent to Heathrow Airport. Nice one.

On my return I was ordered up to the cash office. Oh dear, was I in trouble? No! I had not claimed my overseas allowance of £30 per day. My other expenses were OK…During this period I was working on the DH Comet 4B a modification was ordered to strengthen the wings. This was so complicated that technicians from de Havilland Hatfield were sent out to Nairobi to assist us with this work, which entailed fixing huge plates near the main spars.

I enjoyed working for East African Airways the technical staff were a mixture of European (British) Asians and Africans. The workforce was divided basically thus: - British were aircraft technicians, Asians, aircraft upholsterers, African Nationals were unskilled helpers or labourers. When I commenced employment I was assigned a young African lad. He followed me all day and was on hand if or when I required assistance. One lunch time we were sitting outside the hangar watching aircraft manoeuvring on the airfield when our attention was focused on a Vickers Viscount. It was on take-off and reached the no point of no return down the runway. This is the point when an aircraft must take off or abort safely before running out of runway. There was a huge cloud of smoke and a high pitch noise from the props running at high speed in reverse and within an instance fire engines and other rescue vehicles were chasing down the runway. I sent my companion down the airfield to ascertain, from a safe distance, to obtain any news for me. On his return it appeared, that the pilot was not happy about the engines power and aborted, but it was too late. The Viscount had ended up in the bush, nose downwards. The brakes had melted and caused a fire but all passengers and crew were safe. The only casualty was an African who happened to be in the area, and being inquisitive had walked in to contra rotating spinning propellers.

It was an exciting day when a flight of RAF Gloucester Javelin fighter/bombers landed at Embakasi Airport. This was in response to Ian Smith's declaring Unilateral Declaration of independence (UDI) in Rhodesia (Zimbabwe) on 11th November 1965 after many meetings with the then UK prime minister Harold Wilson to stop a white rule. One African told me at this time, "You English will be fighting yourselves soon", with a laugh.

This must have been about the time of the wind of change blowing through Africa.

I still have a cinema ticket from the "Kenya" cinema in Nairobi dated 6th February 1966. This must have been my last visit to a cinema in Kenya before coming back to the UK.

Near the end of my life in Kenya I travelled from Nairobi to Mombasa by Train. The East African Railways & Harbours Train left Nairobi before sunset and arrived in Mombasa after breakfast the next day. I was shown to my compartment where I was to sleep and the location of the dining car for an evening meal and breakfast. The journey was slow with a double Garrett steam engine powered by oil. During the night I was awoken because we had come to a halt, with a herd of elephants on the line ahead. With much horn blowing over a half hour the herd slowly moved off into the bush. After breakfast we reached Mombasa Station where I was met by Peter Grayson who had left the army to work in Mombasa. I stayed some weeks with Peter and his wife Mary. Oh, happy days.

Later in 1966, just before the World Cup, I re-located back to the United Kingdom to take up an appointment as Training Officer with Metal Propellers Limited, Croydon, Surrey. During the flight back to the UK I had to struggle with my mind, was I doing the right thing. Eventually I saw sense.

In this new post I had to travel from Croydon to Cowes Isle of Wight about once a month because the first-year apprentices had their basic training at Saunders Roe on the island. Like I had done 8 years previously in my own apprenticeship. On one occasion I was returning from Cowes when I decided to travel via the Southampton/Waterloo in a first-class Pullman coach steam train. This must have been the one of the last all Pullman steam trains on this route. Being single and well paid I took every chance to live as I did in East Africa. (Bwana Mkubwa). It took me some time to settle down in England but still wondered if I had made the right decision. Looking back on life since, it transpired I'd made the right choice. However, one of the biggest changes was the reduction of the railway system throughout England in the 1960's by Dr Beeching MP. I have one of the last railway tickets numbered 7119 issued at

Great Yeldham Essex station for the journey to Haverhill Suffolk dated 30th December 1961 which was given to me by Fred Sale who was an ex-Colne Valley railway worker.

Mum & Dad at cousin Sally Mackridge's Wedding

The Industrial Training Boards had been implemented in 1964 by the Labour Government forcing companies to organise training by a system of paying a tax and then claiming grants back for training which had been professional organised. The firm I had been apprenticed to contacted me in Africa with a job offer. Kenya had just become Independent. I guessed it wouldn't be too long before nationals will be employed to a greater degree. It took me a long time to settle down to UK life as I have quoted. I was sent on a six months' residential course at a Southsea hotel near Portsmouth to learn all about this new government training act and training in general. I came really involved and became a founder member The Institution of Training Officers. This was mainly due to an old friend Vic Stevenson the apprentice supervisor at Saunders Roe Limited who was well in to improving his station in life. I enjoyed going to East Cowes and on one occasion I had the privilege to get a trip on the Solent in a small experimental hovercraft. Unfortunately, the jet turbine engine suffered from a flame out and left us stranded mid Solent. The captain of a passing Isle of Wight ferry hailed us, asking if we needed assistance. Our "pilot" replied," No thank you" to my surprise. The engine was fired up again by internal power. This was a design fault with the small hovercraft, having an air intake so low that water on occasions entered the engine and cut the power.

The position of Training Officer back at my old company was fine, but I was still treated as the boy. I had to get out and find another employer who wanted an industrial training officer.

My father had retired from Guy's Hospital and he and Mother had moved to Great Cornard, Sudbury, Suffolk. I lived with them in 1967 and found a position as a Training Officer with Whitlock Brothers Limited at Great Yeldam, Essex. I was to act as their Training Officer shadowing Fred Sale, the Personnel Manager, who was nearing retirement. It was part of the agreement of my employment that I became the company Personnel Manager after he had retired.

Whitlock Brothers Limited was a well-established family business manufacturer of excavators, (Dinkum Diggers), like JCB's. With a great export market employing over 600 personnel it seemed a good place to work. In the past the company had made farm trailers and many implements for the farming industry.

On my first day with Whitlock Bros. I noticed a promotional picture in the Reception of a Whitlock Digger at work at Heathrow Airport and in the background was an East African Airways Comet complete with an air hostess, who I recognised, ferrying passengers on to their flight to Nairobi. It's small world.

Fred Sale was a Magistrate and police officers regularly came to our office with paperwork, and summons requiring his signature.

I got to know the local police very well, and one day a police Sergeant asked me if I would like to join the special constabulary, as he could do with a man of my experience.

Well, after being sworn in at Castle Hedingham Court House and attending Essex Police Headquarters Chelmsford to obtain my uniform, truncheon, whistle and notebook, etc. my career started in the Special Constabulary which lasted 26 years, that's 11 years with Essex Police Force and 15 years with Suffolk Constabulary. I was back in uniform for the fourth time. I was amazed to note that the buttons on my greatcoat were inscribed "Southend on Sea Constabulary". Due to smaller constabulary's amalgamating over the years Essex Police Force must have been using equipment still in their clothing stores. I still have these buttons as a souvenir.

My experiences as a Special Constable are included later in my memories.

Wedding Day 24th February, 1968

I can remember asking Fred Sale, "Who types our letters and paperwork", Fred replied that he didn't have a secretary, but a girl called Gladys in the Production Stores Office was good at shorthand and typing and quite helpful. Well, I got on very well dictating my letters to Gladys and we were married on 24th February 1968, three months after our first meeting in the office.

    I had been so busy in my life that married life was going to pass me by at the age of 30 years. My mother enquired one morning when was I going to find a nice girl and get married. She said I would end up a dirty old man if I didn't marry and settle down. Well, I had let her down by not taking holy orders, I better get married. The first young lady I met that morning was Gladys. We now have two girls, Michele born 13th December 1968, and Lynda a born 6th October, 1971 plus Robin born 18th October 1972. Four grandchildren, two girls, Emily and Lucy and three boys Jamie, Liam, Ryan and one great grandson Jaiden,

Of course, I must not forget our son and daughter- in -laws: - Lynda married Jerry Godden and Robin married Jackie Washbourn.

Whitlock Digger working at Heathrow with DH Comet in background

During this period, I became Secretary/Treasurer to The Great Yeldham Educational Foundation, Clerk to the Great Yeldham and Stoke-by-Clare Parish Councils, Treasurer to the Great Yeldham United Charities and a Special Constable. I was keen to understand and work with the local community. I was Secretary/Treasurer to the Great Yeldham Education Foundation for about 30 years. On one occasion near the end of this period I have a story to tell. The trustees wanted to transfer a sum of money from one saving account to another Post Office account which offered a higher interest rate. I applied for this to be done, and the bankers asked for the original trustee's signatures at the time of opening this account to sign a document to release the funds for transfer. Well, all the original trustees were dead. I therefore informed the bank that these trustees were dead but they still insisted they signed the Forms. After speaking to the present trustees, they were unhelpful. I had no option but to forge the signatures of the dead trustees, and the money was therefore transferred to the account that the present trustees wish.

I was worried about my action for some time, as an up standing person of the community and a constable of the County. But it was the bad system that caused the situation. Happy days. I attended a meeting of the National Association of Parish Clerks in London on one occasion. I remember meeting the Little Yeldham Parish Council Clerk, Adrian Corder-Birch the son of "Bunny" Birch" an employee of Whitlock Bros. Adrian has written a book of the history of the Whitlock Bros. Factory in Great Yeldham.

As a Personnel Manger I witnessed how different human-beings operated and treat one another. Every time we employed a person who we did not know, we had to ring a telephone number to enquire if they were known as a trouble maker. If the reply was "not known", they could be employed. I was also in contact with other personnel managers in the area to ensure wage rates were the same and kept in line with local agreed rates. We always checked the suitability of unknown applicants. When Works Union employees tried to inform me that such in such company's rates were higher, I could ensure them they weren't with impunity.

I had a "surgery" every lunch time for employee's problems.

One man asked me for advance on his wages every week. One week I refused. Later I received a telephone call from a local communist councillor saying why I hadn't given this man a sub. I stated that if he couldn't handle his money, like everyone else he would continue asking for subs for the rest of his life. The councillor stated that we have to look after these poor people who can't budget for themselves. I suggested the councillor give this man advice on handling his weekly wage and I would approve one more advance. I never heard any more from her or the man.

During this period 1973 to 1975 the Vietnamese War was being fought. "Tie a yellow ribbon round the old oak tree".

Being a Personnel Manager I learnt how to negotiate with the convenor and the local union representatives. I had my secretary in at management and union meetings taking down what was said in short hand and then getting union members present to sign a typed copy as prove of our conversation. This stopped any arguments regarding the spoken word. This sometimes proved most invaluable. I often wondered what motivated a person to become a shop steward or in fact a Member of Parliament. This worried me because most were sincere to their cause, but others were hunting for self-praise. If a shop steward was needed by a group of workers, most of them would duck down under the parapet, and only the one wanting self-praise would put him or herself forward for election, and mostly got appointed unopposed.

I found dealing with people very satisfying and interesting.

I spent eight fruitful years at Great Yeldham. In 1972 Powell Duffryn bought Whitlocks Bros. and incorporated it with Hy-Mac and eventually the bubble burst. In 1974 I was asked to make over 500 employees redundant over a 12-month period.

Then, wait for it, make myself redundant in May 1975 with an added bonus of £200.00. Hy-Mac did make me an offer of employment in South Wales as a junior personnel officer. After great thought I declined this offer. As an English personnel officer in South Wales where most of the employees were Welsh, I didn't think it was a good idea. We had a lovely week's holiday by the Norfolk coast before I returned to make myself redundant.

This was a coming to be a very low point, no job and a family to support.

We were now living in Stoke by Clare, Suffolk in a small cottage. which was advertised for £5,500, I offered £5,000 and it was accepted. I brought it for cash after selling the home in Sible Hedingham at great profit.

I was asked if I would like to be Clerk to the Stoke-by-Clare Parish Council for a small sum, as I had good experience in this field, I took the position on. There were not many suitable full-time jobs in the area at the time.

A retired lady living in the village asked me if I could re-upholster a chair for her, I hired a small barn and got to work. I always confirmed, that if you can handle one type material like metal the same principles apply to fabric. or any other material in fact, that is: - "Mark out, cut, form, and join. The chair was successful, and I was paid £70.

There was an office chair manufacturer in Haverhill, called Project Office Furniture. A friend, of mine, Rod Gibson was a great help to go with me cap in hand, asking if we could help them with any production work that they could not manage. They replied by stating that they were sending access production up to the Midlands as there wasn't any suitable upholsterer locally, so if we could prove ourselves the contract was ours. We managed to find a chap in Haverhill who had worked for the Company and he completed a sampler for us.

The sample, was prefect, as you might expect and we got the contract. The managing director's name was "Bardesly". I asked him if he was related to the late Archbishop of Coventry Cathedral Dr Cuthbert Bardesly who was related to an elder priest, Rev. Bardsley of St. John's the Evangelist of Upper Norwood. SE19. "No" was the reply.

Now, I had to get the upholstery equipment and tools. I contacted an upholstery supplier in East London. They sent a representative to see me. He was a great help and let me have equipment on 30 days' credit. I picked his brain on upholstery procedures then managed to employ three staff on a self-employment basis and trained the ones that had not been employed by the local upholstery company.

We turned over many of hundred pounds each month it was great fun. However, I over worked myself and ended up suffering from exhaustion. The doctor told me to take it easy. I did by letting the staff run the business and I used our works van to do work for a local contract carpet company. It was mainly delivering carpet stands to exhibitions around the country and returning them when the show was over. I went as far as Glasgow once and slept in the van.

My younger sister, Jasmine lived in Dovercourt, near Harwich. Her husband Michael Coffey worked at Warners' Holiday Camp. With Michaels help I secured an annual contract that lasted many years recovering the Holiday Camp seating. I learnt from a friend, Ken Overman, that this holiday camp was used to accommodate the Kinder Transport that organised Jewish children from Germany before the war in 1939 when the camp was empty prior to the next holiday season. Ken himself has a great story to tell regarding his life escaping from the Nazi party, joining the British Army Tank Corps and eventually settling in England after the war. Another interesting fact is that the comedy series broadcast on TV called Hi de Hi was mainly filmed at this very same Warner's Holiday Camp.

One of my staff, Julius Bell, had seen an advertisement in the London Evening News seeking for upholsterers to work in Saudi Arabia. I applied, and after two months, I had a telephone call stating that the agents for the Saudi Arabia contract had now recruited sufficient upholsterers, but however, would I be interested in hemming and hanging curtains in a Riyadh Palace.

"Yes." I replied "Good, can you commence in two days' time, we will organise your flight to Riyadh".

The only other person who was interested in accompanying me was my brother-in-law Phillip Shinn. We travelled to the head office of the company who were contracting us at Hounslow west London for finial instructions. Then a taxi to Heathrow airport. The flight was uneventful, we stopped at Jeddah and were ordered off the aircraft for custom checks, then ordered on to continue to Riyadh. A Local overseer met us at the airport and took us to a palace. Most of the work was simple. Hanging curtains, measuring the drop and hemming the bottom which was made difficult due to the inner lining, and the blackout lining to reduce heat in the room. We spent five weeks in Riyadh, and learnt how to hem and hang curtains on the job. We were accommodated in the servant's quarters of the palace where we were working. It was a very boring job and nowhere to for a break at the end of the day, as it was in the middle of a desert. However, the overseer did take us all out for a meal one evening at a restaurant in Riyadh once. We had a good evening with super food. The sweet, a Swiss dish was called Tete a tete, a large glass bowl full of all types of fresh fruits and ice creams, which went down very nicely. I bet the assembled company that I could eat one whole fruit bowl. The money was placed on the table and I commenced eating. I love ice cream and fruit so this was going to be easy. After 15 minutes I was finding it hard. The other diners began smiling and holding their spoons with anticipation. I was absolutely stuffed and gave up and lost £30. We had a good evening and as you may imagine not a drop of alcohol to drink due to Saudi Arabian Laws. We were also invited to the overseer's bungalow one evening for eats and fruit juices. On the ride back to the palace I came a little suspicious, I was a little merry, perhaps the fruit juices had been spiked with alcohol. On return to UK my young children were over the moon to see their daddy again with money stuffed in all my pockets.

The office chair contract lasted several years, but my mistake was not to get out into the market place and find additional work in case things went belly up.

After a holiday in the Highlands, I returned to find the staff idle.

The contract had finished due to a national industrial depression. I had no other work and had to stopped trading. This taught me a great lesson, when in business always keep your eye on the ball and do not rely on one contract. Earning a living, being self-employed and bringing up a young family is very an important to get it right.

Freemasonry

I had been interested in freemasonry from an early age, and remember as a choirboy hearing the mature male members of the choir talking about freemasonry whist we were in the vestry before services. My maternal grandad had been a Freemason also some of my paternal uncles. Uncle William A. Mackridge was a keen Freemason and a member of Edgware Lodge No. 3866 became Worshipful Master in 1966. He attended my Initiation on Tuesday 11th March, 1980 at Royal Clarence Lodge No. 1823 Clare Suffolk.

I became Worshipful Master of the Lodge on 10th October, 1995.

The Ladies' Festival was held at Clare Town Hall on the 27th April 1996. 1996 was a busy year for our family, not only for the Ladies Festival, but Lynda married Jerry Godden on 1st June and also Robin married Jackie 30th March. Jerrys' father was the Assistant Provincial Grand Master of Cambridgeshire so I was a regular visitor to a few Cambridgeshire lodges.

In 1999 I joined East & Central Africa Lodge No. 7446 and became their Master on July 2011. When I was Master of Royal Clarence Lodge, I met many masters of other lodges in Suffolk, one such Master was John Pimm of Babergh No. 8122. John had also worked in East Africa attached to a bank and introduced me to the East & Central Africa Lodge. The members of this lodge were from or had connections in east or central Africa. It amazed me that although religion was not mentioned in lodges, this lodge was made up of many religious sets, for example: - Christians, Hindus, Jews, Muslims etc. and we all worked and relaxed together in complete harmony. All the members of East & Central Africa Lodge are very caring and they have helped me in sickness and health over the years. Many names that come to mind are Dilip Patel, Jignish Patel, Rashmi Patel, Minish Patel, Shammeer Shah, Jim Wallace, Pradip Patel Snr, Pridip Patel Jnr. Aunali & Imran Jaffer, Don MacLean, Harihar Patel, and lots more. Harihar and Rashmi invited me to another Lodge which happened to be Edgware Lodge, my Uncle Wills Mackridge's Lodge. The Edgware Lodge members treated me as a great friend instantly. I have made many friends by attending my own and other lodges.

Since 2017 I have been honorary Outer Guard or Tyler to three lodges in Saffron Walden which are: - Walden Lodge No. 1280, Stedfast Unity Lodge No. 9128 and Lux Solis Lodge No. 9781. Lux Solis is a day light lodge because it meets at 12 noon. For these duties I get paid a small sum and a free supper. It also gave me the added advantage of meeting another circle of fresh friends.

Amongst many are, Gerald Smith (no relation but an ex-employee of Whitlock Bros.), Headley O'Brien, Keith Huddlestone, Tony Batchelor, Peter Telford, Roger Kendrick, Paul Beaufils, Douglas Kent, Dennis Stratton, Graham Newstead, Evan Grant and many more. Freemasonry helps those in distress nationwide and also with local charities. I find it relaxing, great fun and the corps de sprit is great. All types representing society become Freemasons. I joined the following "side Degrees: - Royal Clarence, Royal Arch on the 20th March 1985, Simon of Sudbury Chapter Rose Croix on the 22nd April. 1996; and Mark Mason including Ark Mariners on the 24th January, 1997. One occasion I remember as a family attachment, I was attending Cambridge Guildhall to witness Chris Godden, my daughter Lynda's father-in-law, invested as Deputy Provincial Grand Master of Cambridgeshire. I met many friends from all over East Anglia.

Each lodge has its own unique history, meeting technique, rituals and standards.

I find there is a great difference between lodges on how the welfare of the members is looked after. This is due to the wide type of the member's personality and social standing all acting at the same level in a common way.

Some lodges are so laid back and relaxed with their work while others are so strict it is almost too serious. However, either way it is very interesting and I always have a good night.

Saffron Walden being a Quaker town there is a Friend's lodge and they have a great custom after meetings. If anyone wants to say anything they must stand up and tell the assembled company.

You can imagine how many amusing stories and jokes are told.

An archbishop once referred to freemasonry as a bunch of over grown schoolboys having fun. Most elderly members attend meetings continuously until they join the Grand Architect above.

East & Central Africa Lodge No.7446

Worshipful Master:
W. Bro. Eldon Mackridge PPGS of W (Suffolk)

Installation Dinner
5th July 2011

Festive Board

A New Life and Experiences with TWI

When I was apprenticed to Metal Propellers Limited the company were members of the Welding Institute in Great Abingdon. Each year The Welding Institute had an open day for their members.

The Welding Foreman and General Manager of Metal Propellers usually attended this event. But one year the General Manager could not attend and asked the Foremen to take an apprentice. I was told I was going on this jolly. It was not really long after WW2 1955 and I had not seen so much wonderful food in my life. I always remember this day and when the Welding Institute job came up, I knew it was for me. (It's a small world).

The Welding Institute were advertising for a Chauffeur at the time my upholstery company closed for business, I applied and was successful engaged. Now started another chapter in my working life. I liked travelling, driving and meeting people so going to work was a happy experience. People who lived for the weekend and dreaded Mondays in their life seemed a poor bunch to me, I always loved my work.

Being chauffeur to the top management and the scientists I quickly
came to know the important members of staff and the work they carried out. There was a lot of travel to all major airports and engineering businesses and universities in the UK.

Some of the scientific language I heard was familiar regarding the scholarly stainless-steel properties, austenitic and martensitic which I leant about during my apprenticeship days at Metal Propellers Limited.

I could write a book about my experiences driving people around. I was discreet then as well as now. However, I can tell some stories of an anonymous nature. Amusing occasions that come to mind hereby follow: -

If I had a pickup in central London early in the morning, I'd always drive to London very, very early to miss the rush hour traffic and sit in the car near to the hotel reading a book etc. One cold morning I was some distance from the hotel and wanted to relieve myself, I always had an empty whisky bottle in the car for such occasions. I nearly filled the bottle and placed the cork in it and dropped the bottle into a handy placed waste bin attached to a lamp post adjunct to the car.

I dosed off and was awoken by a tramp rummaging in the waste bin, his eyes sparkling with glee as he gasped my whisky bottle and made a swift walk down the road. I often wonder what his reaction would be like when he made a sip of my "Scotch".

This experience really tickled Ron Edwards, a co chauffeur, when I told him this story. Ron and Ginny Edwards or the "Weasleys as my daughter Lynda called them.

One evening the company were having a meeting at a top hotel in London. When I arrived with the directors the staff were already at the hotel organising the event. As I dropped the top men and women off I enquired what time they wanted to be collected for the return trip. The Doorman whispered in my ear, don't worry you can park in the hotel car park for free.

I then walked into the reception, a lady member who was attending the event on seeing me, asked how I was going to pass the time until my boss wanted to go home. As she was staying the night, she thought it a good idea if I took the key to her room and then I could make a cup of tea or coffee and watch TV until the event finished. Thanking her I found the room via the number on the key.

Settled down with a nice cup of tea watching TV. It was about 8 pm when I heard a most unusual noise coming from the adjoining room, through the rather thin walls. Quick I thought someone needs medical help, I rang reception stating that someone in the next room needed a doctor or ambulance. The receptionist calmed me down and said, would I monitor the noises and report back to her as she did not want to have an unnecessary alarm.

I listened for some time and then it dawned on me what the noises were.

I turned the TV volume up and settled down again. After about 30 minutes the room telephone rang, the receptionists said, "Do you still want a doctor". "NO! NO! All is OK", I said, thank you for your help. It never crossed my mind that such intimate things went on so early in the evening.

Several jobs I did were unofficial like collecting children of staff from school, staff to London Theatres, Horse Racing, Office romance trips and weddings. I had to keep my mouth shut and not see or hear what was happening in the rear-view mirror. I even had a woman doing a complete dress and underwear change behind me, with much amusement to lorry drivers looking down into the rear of my car.

I drove members of parliament, titled people and their families and of course Bevan Braithwaite OBE the CEO of The Welding Institution. The chauffeurs I subcontracted were: - Malcolm Bailey, Ron Edwards, Ibrahim Guru Cadenza (a Turkish business man/chauffeur commonly known as "Freedom"), and Martin England a retired Suffolk Constabulary police officer and many others. We had great fun working together, always getting the jobs done in a very professional way and I was never let down by them.

As I said previously, I could write a book about these experiences but I think this is bad practice. I was in the customers' private life due to my employment and it wasn't for me to tell anyone else about what I heard or saw.

I worked for TWI until I was 65 years old, took my staff pension, then worked until 75 years old in a self-employed capacity.

I met other drivers at airports and horse racing events around the UK making friends with many drivers, trainers and horse dealers.

If we weren't invited into the events, the drivers had their own picnics and tote bets in the car parks and enjoyed the camaraderie of exchanging stories. One such friend was Malcolm Bailey who I mention earlier, introduced many clients to me.

During this period of self-employment, I applied for and was successful in obtaining a part time contract driving the solicitor in charge of Mills & Reeves, Duncan Ogilvy. It was basically a Wednesday job. Whereby I drove Duncan Ogilvy to the Mills & Reeve branch in Birmingham every Wednesday in their vehicle. Mills Reeves had litigation contracts with the NHS so I drove Duncan to many hospitals in the Midlands then back to Cambridge for about three years. I really enjoyed this work and Duncan showed his appreciation by asking me to drive both his daughters on their respective wedding days. I learnt a lot from Duncan and I think he learnt a bit from me about life. "Happy days".

Another long-term contract was driving Richard Warburton and occasional his staff to and from London Airports, and other addresses in the UK in his rather nice four-wheel drive Audi 6 Quarto.

I must record a funny experience whilst working for Richard Warburton. Richard asked me to meet him at a location in Leicestershire where he would be attending a funeral at a church in the grounds of a manor house, and then, after the service drive him to Gatwick Airport. I found the said property and drove up the drive to the house to wait for the attendees to complete their refreshments and farewells. To make myself clear for Richard to see me, I stood by the entrance hall in my smart suit. After a while people started to leave, approaching me and shaking my hand and thanking me, stating that my house was so beautiful. It didn't deem the occasion to correct them, so I enjoyed the moment of being the lord of the manor.

One day I drove a person to Ely Cathedral for a meal. When I returned after the event I parked by a smart Range Rover, to await for my passenger. I got chatting to the driver and it soon became apparent he was a chauffeur to the Royals. I was surprised when HRH Prince Philip approached and said good evening to me, jumped into the Range Rover and was gone. There was no police backup and the local police only passed once while I was talking to the chauffeur. Very low key.

CRIMESTOPPERS VOLUNTEER GOES THE EXTRA MILE AND RAISES £900 FOR THE CHARITY

A PROACTIVE Crimestoppers volunteer from Haverhill, Suffolk, has driven from Lands End to John O'Groats in a Crimestoppers branded car to raise much needed funds for the independent crime-fighting charity.

Eldon Mackridge, Secretary of Royal Clarence Lodge, No 1823, meeting in Clare, was the fundraiser and Suffolk Crimestoppers volunteer. He turned 75 in September and took on the drive for his birthday. The 850 mile journey from Cornwall to the Scottish Highlands kicked off on 8th September from Lands End and took 3 days to complete.

Prior to the expedition Eldon stayed in a bed and breakfast the night before just 12 miles from the starting point. In an act of utter coincidence the venue, which Eldon chose at random, was owned by someone who used to be chair of an East Midlands Volunteer Committee some years ago. Eldon remarked: "Crimestoppers is such a small charity with only six-hundred volunteers UK wide, so it really was amazing to stumble across another supporter."

The first night was spent in Gloucester and the second night was spent in Perth, with a race to the finish at John O'Groats the next day at 2.30pm.

Crimestoppers Eastern Regional Manager, Ann Scott, said: "This was a great initiative thought up by Eldon. We are so grateful for the lengths our volunteers go to in order to raise our profile. Eldon is raising money for Crimestoppers so that we can continue to fight crime and make a difference in our community. Many people do not realise that we are an independent charity, but think we are part of the police or the TV programme. We need to raise funds in order to promote the vital anonymous service that we provide and pay the rewards available for information given to us."

She added: "With 23 arrests being made every day from information given to Crimestoppers the charity plays a significant part in getting criminals off the street. The charity has many active and passionate volunteers, like Eldon, who give up their own time to promote the charity. If you would like to support Crimestoppers by volunteering you can find more information by visiting www.crimestoppers-uk.org."

Eldon commented: "I am very pleased with the amount of money raised - you always worry that you won't raise a penny! There is still time to donate and help fight crime in Suffolk. I thoroughly enjoyed the whole experience and I'm already planning my next fundraising adventure."

As a result of this fundraising event The Lands End to John O'Groats Association will be awarding Eldon with a prestigious award for 'Oldest Fundraiser' at their AGM in January.

Suffolk Crimestoppers would like to thank all that donated money via the Just Giving page, the text number and by cash/cheque donations to Eldon. In particular they would like to thank Royal Clarence Charity Association, East & Central Africa Lodge, Pat Hall, David Cousins, Neville Gay, David Cousins and a few anonymous donors. Paragon Signs also kindly branded Eldon's car free of charge. In total Eldon raised over £900.

If you wish to support Eldon's efforts and donate any amount you can spare, please go to www.justgiving.com/SuffolkCrimestoppersDrive.

Suffolk Masonic Magazine cutting

On my 75th birthday I decided to drive from Land's End to John Groats to raise money for the Crimestoppers Charity. Gladys does not drive so it was all down to me, however, she is a first-class navigator and good company. I contacted companies allied to the motor trade for sponsorship. Michelin was the most generous.

We drove from Suffolk to Land's End where we had pre-arranged to stay overnight for bed & breakfast at Marazion overlooking St, Michael's Mount. And guess what, the B&B owner was an ex-policeman and knew some of the staff of Crimestoppers. "It's a small world". Next morning, we travelled to Land's End to commence our end to end. We stopped two nights during the fund-raising trip. The first was on the outskirts of Gloucester 6.75 hours travelling time and the second night just west of Perth 7.75 hours. The third day to John Groats 5 hours 20 minutes. Arriving at 2:40pm. Total mileage 854 miles. We raised just under £10,00.00 for the Crimestoppers Charity. Many people do not realise that Crimestoppers is a charity that passes information gained anonymously from an informant on to the police and often pay a sum of money to the informant. We achieved a vast amount of publicity during our end to end, which was most encouraging. I met a local gentleman carrying vegetables from his allotment and on seeing the Crimestoppers logos on my car said, "You want to catch some of the villains around here". I was surprised that there was a crime wave in John O'Groats. "Yes", he said, "I moved here after retiring from the Metropolitan Police to get away from crime and find crime is here, but on a much smaller scale".

The following year we completed a trip organised by the Lands End John O'Groats Association in the reverse order from John O'Groats to Land's End to mark their 30th anniversary. This was not to raise funds for any charities, but it gave us a chance to meet other members of the Association and have a jolly good time with likeminded people.

LEJOG Association have their AGM every year at Torquay.
Gladys and I have attended everyone since 2008.
On one of the AGM meetings at Torquay, Gladys and I sat next to Geoff and Ann De'Ath for dinner. The subject of our conversation got round to surnames and Geoff stated that he knew of a Mackridge family who were related to him by marriage. By cross examining Geoff, it appeared that this connection with a Mackridge was

through a brother of my father's Uncle Will & Aunt Middy who lived in Mill Hill, London with their two off springs, John and Sally. It's a small world!

I am now Social Secretary of the Land's End John O'Groats Association, organising the AGM at Torquay and another late summer weekend at different locations throughout the British Isles late each year. It is great fun organising the AGM and a late summer event each year.

Gladys and I have met a new circle of friends by joining LEJOG Association. One particular was Cliff Harrison also a craftsman who served in R.E.M.E for his National Service, unfortunately he passed away in 2017. He made a clock to remind me of my service life. We had a lot in common and had great fun reminiscing about our service days as Craftsmen. Cliff's wife and daughter Sue still attend the AGM at Torquay and our late summer events. Brian Dawson the Chairman and his wife Pat are a great help to me and we seemed to work very well together at a committee level. Other new friends include Jack & Theresa Adams, Rob Willis, Val Beckett, Susan Liechti (from Switzerland), Steve Gibbs, Don & Jean Dyer, Des & Frankie Bass to name a few.

Serving the Queen again as a Special Constable.

During my 26 years from 27th April 1971 to 9th September 1997 with the Special Constabulary I had many interesting experiences with different classes of people living in Essex and Suffolk.   In the early days it was catching poachers and petty thieves.   Later I enjoyed the chase, with blue lights and sirens. Most "shouts" were OK to deal with, but when children were involved in accidents and injured it was very sad and upsetting as I had young children of my own. I always was glad that the ambulance staff were in attendance or not too far away. I take my hat off to these medics. When returning home after a tour of duty it always took me some time to calm down due to the hype.

Here are some of my lighter hearted experiences: -

I remember one evening 6th October, 1971 in Essex, news came in that person's unknown were breaking into a school at night in Sible Hedingham. We were dispatched in our Minivan to the school to make observations. After about an hour of boring idleness we saw some movement in the dark. We crept into the school corridor and witnessed a person in the head master's office. My colleague whispered, "Quick, now is your chance for a collar.". I crept into the office, my heart beating like mad. The thief was bending over an open desk draw unaware I was right behind him. I placed my hand on his shoulder, stating "You are nicked". The thief went stiff with fright, and I was about the same with adrenalin coursing through my body. It was easy when you apply surprise tactics, I thought handing him over to the Custody Sergeant at the Halstead nick. I remember this night very well because Gladys was at Bury St. Edmunds hospital in labour, and as I came off duty, I was called to attend the Hospital urgently. I witnessed my daughter; Lynda being born with me still in uniform with much happiness and congratulations to my wife and the policeman from the hospital maternity staff.

Whilst serving with Essex Police I was called on duty one Saturday evening to Halstead Court House where there were about twenty police officers under the charge of Chief Inspector David Le Voire. It appeared that Halstead police were having trouble with Braintree youths entering Halstead night spots and fighting with Halstead youths. We were briefed regarding a dance in a hall where it was believed the Braintree youths would start a fight.

After some hours we were sent into action in police transit vans with orders from the Chief Inspector that he would lead with a charge with the regulars and then specials backing them up. We charged into the hall and into the youths without using our truncheons unless needed. The youths withdrew at a great pace through all of the emergency exits. The Braintree gang jumped into their cars and headed back to Braintree where their local police were waiting for them. I am glad to say no arrests or injuries sustained.

Chelmsford Essex Police Headquarters annual parade 1970; s

I had not been a special constable very long in the Essex Police when I attended an annual parade for all Essex Specials at police headquarters Springfield Chelmsford. The inspecting Officer was Douglas Bader, the famous WW11 fighter pilot with tin legs. As he approached the rear file where I was standing to attention, he slowed and advanced to me and said, "Where are your medals, officer". I replied, "I haven't got any, Sir". He said "Never mind, you will soon have one". I include a photograph taken on that occasion with my section, unfortunately Douglas Bader did not get in the picture but our group from Castle Hedingham Police Station look a team to be reckoned with in the 1970's. Notice that we have not got diced bands around our caps at this stage. It was thought that police officers would stand out from all the other men in uniform i.e., like milkman, gasman, bus conductors & drivers etc. So, this cap band was taken from the Scottish police, who had always had a diced band which was copied from the Scottish soldier's bonnet years before. Now the diced band is found in all emergency services like ambulance personal and vehicles. The City of London Police are exception having worn a red diced band.

One late night we were mobile in the Police Minivan when we came across a car, miles from anywhere in the Steeple-Bumpstead Thaxted area parked on the grass verge which looked unattended. My police driver asked me to check it out. As I approached the said car two people half undressed popped up, "What's going on here", I said, not knowing what to say in such a funny situation. The male said "I'm just teaching my secretary how to drive, officer". "OK, goodnight sir, drive carefully", I replied. No offence committed I told my colleague.

An interesting 'shout' was to a noisy party, neighbours had complained by reporting to the police of a late noisy party.
   On arrival we were invited into the property, I recognised a male party-goer, as my bank manager. He came embarrassed and quickly tried to inform the other policemen present and the party goers that he was a great friend of mine and no action should be taken. That was the worst thing he could try to establish, suitable advice was given, and we left. Next morning, I changed banks, I couldn't face that man again.

One day in a police station I was asked to change into civvies and join an identification parade line up. The suspect was in the line of civilian volunteers with me in the charge room. The lady witness came into the room with the detectives, the she whispered, "That one", pointing at me. You can imagine the ribbing I had for some time for being "recognised" in an identification parade as a criminal.
   We were quite often required to do under cover duties in commercial premises after working hours watching for crimes and then alerting uniform patrols to attend. Sometimes, in the industrial areas watching in case of break ins or watching the high street during weekend evenings in case of vandalism. On one occasion when we were posted on a flat roof of a bank overlooking a High Street to spy on trouble makers. I was called to assist uniform officers trying to arrest a trouble maker in front of a large plate glass shop window. The officers were on each side of the youth, "Quick" they said "Grab him". Not knowing where to grab him I bent down and lifted one of the youth's feet up as high as possible causing him to lose his balance and fall against the shop window with such a force that we all broke the window and shower of glass came down

on us. I told the Sergeant I was responsible for breaking a shop window. "Don't worry, I've charged the trouble maker for resisting arrest and criminal damage", said the custody sergeant with a smile.

We were always called out for carnivals, and fêtes. With carnivals parading through the town all cars parked must be removed to allow free movement of the procession. It was quite easy to identify the owners by knocking on doors. However, one day we could not find an owner of a parked car, so I contacted the police national computer to establish the owner. The reply surprised me. The car had been stolen many days previously from London. The local residents had not reported this car in their road as unknown. Also, the local Beat Officers' had not noticed it as a stolen vehicle. Most embarrassing!

We had a great laugh one evening, an officer was bragging that he had attended all crimes possible except a sudden death.

When he was out of the office another officer and myself set up a "sudden death scenario". He was about to go off duty, he went home and organised for his wife to contact the police station knowing that our "victim" was in the office answering incoming phone calls.

Our "victim officer" said to me you stay here; I've got a sudden death to attend to in the town you organise the Coroners Officer to attend. The next I heard was that our friend got to the address. A lady opened the door sobbing saying her husband was in the bedroom on the bed under a sheet. Our friend went upstairs into the bedroom pulled the sheet back and the officer jumped up with a loud shout "YOUR FIRST SUDDEN DEATH!". You can imagine the poor officers state and the leg pulling on his return to the police station.

As time went on social attitudes changed and I'm sorry to say the police did not change quick enough to keep pace with those changes. Instead of being an officer in uniform to be respected, it was them and us.

A lost hound dog was brought into the Police Office, I recorded the details and took the dog to the police station kennels.

Several days later the head of the local hunt arrived to claim the dog. I happened to be on duty and remembered the dog. I asked the owner for a sight of the dog licence. He replied "I do not have one". I read him his rights and charged him for not having a dog licence. Many days later I was called to the Chief Inspectors office and informed that hunt dogs do not need licences and my charge was being revoked. I didn't win that one.

Now one of the most bizarre: -

I was on duty on one Sunday afternoon with the Steeple Bumpstead's detached officer, Pc Ken Marks, when we were asked to attend a 999 call from a gentleman living in Bures (about 19 miles away from our location) reporting vandalism. Bures in those days had two police stations, one in Essex for Essex Police and the other in Suffolk for Suffolk Constabulary due the border being in Bures on both sides of the river. The detached officers were not contactable on either side of the river Stour.

On arrival, the gentleman asked if we wanted a cup of tea or something stronger, we declined, saying please show us the vandalism he wanted to report. Please come into my garage and I will explain. We stood around his car in his cramped garage and he stated that he had attended church that morning, and on leaving church noticed that someone had painted a stripe each side of his new Vauxhall Viva. I bent down to look closer and all I could see was a thin coach line. If someone had painted this on his car whilst he was in church, they had made a very good job of it.

He was insistent that when he brought the car new from the local dealers, in Sudbury, he didn't want any chrome strips or lines down the side of his new car. I didn't know what to think, I even pressed my thumb hard on the coach line and was beginning to think the paint was still wet, which it was not. The gentleman was sure that those lines were not on his car before going into the church. We left him and went to the church to see if there was any prove of evidence. We could not find any sign of the phantom painters having been in action in the location.

Several days later the victim apologised for wasting police time and stated that coach lines must have been on his car, but he had not noticed them. Bright individual!

The older policemen told me many stories; most had served in the Second World War. One of the Castle Hedingham officers "Robbie" who had served in the Royal Navy during the war, told me amusing story when he was on duty and the Queen attended a town hall. He was stationed in front of the main entrance. The Queen and Prince Phillip arrived. The Prince recognised "Robbie's Naval medal as they passed making some remark. After some time, the royal Party came out on to the balcony above the main entrance, the crowd cheered so "Robbie looked up, right up and saw the Queen's pants.

My skipper, in Essex Police, was Special Sergeant Maurice Mansfield had me in fits one day telling me about his life as a special officer in the days without a radio.

A whistle was useless in the country areas so the duty sergeant gave us coins so we could contact the nearest police station by public phone boxes or knock on a farmhouse door and ask to use their phone. I had to use this method once whilst on duty at a Polling Station when a young man was kicking off about the security of the voting system. Members of the public were always very helpful in those days, first door I knocked on even offered me a cup of tea. If the fire or ambulance services were called to a "shout" we were always informed and decided if the police were needed. Once, when attending a factory fire near a residential area a lady offered all the firemen and me tea and biscuits, nice.

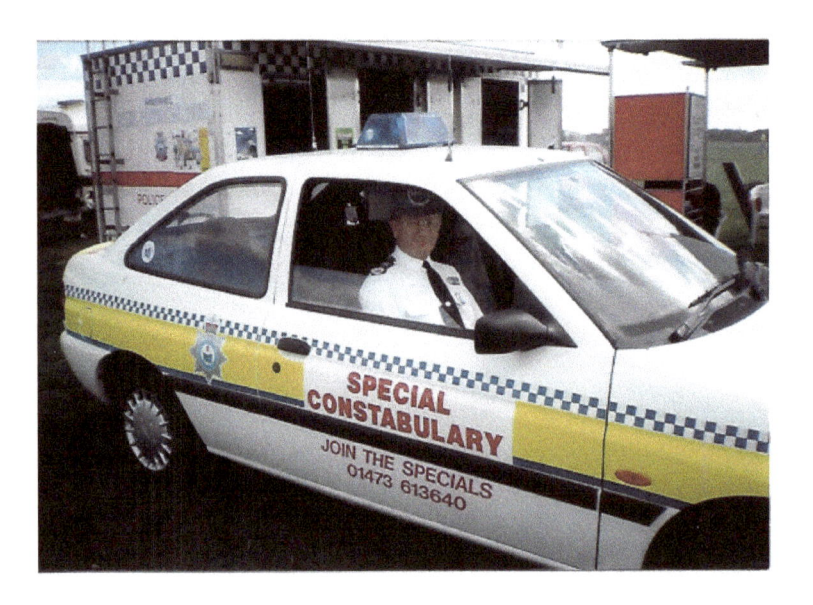

Near the end of my 26 years 'on the job' I was transferred to the Traffic Unit, Bury St. Edmunds which meant double crewing in a big fast traffic car and some unmarked helping motorists, catching speeders, drink drivers, attending to road traffic accidents and assisting the local police towns when required. One evening we were called to an accident on the A14 east bound track. An elderly

German gentleman was trying to travel to Norwich, realising he was going in the wrong direction, tried to do a 'U' turn in front of an HGV. by crossing over the central reservation to the west bound track. Luckily no one was hurt but his car was a right off. I have seen vehicles travelling the wrong way along dual carriageways, motorists physically fighting over who was to blame for a minor accident and had to be restrained, and convened on married couples arguing in their cars in heavy traffic.

We stopped a driver at 5pm one afternoon for a moving traffic violation and asked him if he had been drinking. He answered, "No, officer". So, I said, "Do you mind if you took a specimen of your breath. "No, I haven't had a drink today, go ahead officer", he said with full confidence that he was not drank. The result of the breath test was just under the failure. We asked him again if he had a drink and he replied, "I haven't had a single drink today, but I got plastered last night". Well, that just shows you how long alcohol remains in your body. In this case say midnight to 5pm equals 17 hours. He must had had few.

I include a photograph of a myself and a Haverhill Brownie pack taken by the "Haverhill Echo" newspaper for a police and Crimestoppers initiative teaching children to be aware of all sorts of crime.

I was honoured to receive a Special Constable Medal and later a bar from Her Majesty the Queen for long and faithful service.

A Police Officer once told me, "When you are dealing with people, you are dealing with the abnormal all the time". If you think about this statement it is very true. Policemen deal with all sorts of people and situations which makes their job very satisfying, most of the time. Most members of the population do not come into contact with the police service all their lives, it is only a small majority who are "regular costumers".

When on duty with traffic we were occasionally instructed by the duty sergeant to attend on code name "Brush". This entailed checking on property of a highly important person living in Suffolk.

I was asked to work with the Crime Prevention Officer. We attended the Haverhill and District Crime Prevention Panel meetings. After about a year I was appointed Chairman of the Panel and worked hard to reduce crime in the area. We obtained funding to purchase an unused ex British Telecom mobile display unit, which we converted for our use as mobile Police Crime Prevention Panel Exhibition Unit. Local businesses displayed their logos on the outside of the unit for a fee. We attended most summer fêtes, carnivals, Thurlow Steam Rally, and National Trust open days to advertise crime prevention. The Thurlow Steam Rally was always a good meeting as it was an event over two days. We either locked up the Unit and came home between the two days. or as we did most years borrowed a caravan. As I was still a Special Constable I was provided with a radio in case of any trouble. One night I switched the radio off to get a good night's sleep. In the very early hours, we were awakened by an awful large bang on the door with violent rocking of the caravan. It was the local police night watch checking that all was well. Suffolk Police Headquarters had been trying to contact me via radio with a welfare call each hour, and as I had not responded the local police were engaged to check on us. Luckily no action was taken, but I got a ribbing from my colleagues. Due to cut backs Suffolk Constabulary cut funding and the Crime Prevention Panels closed down. I carried on as Chairman to the local Neighbourhood Watch Schemes in South Haverhill. I still attend the Suffolk Neighbourhood Watch Association AGM meetings. I became a volunteer member of Crimestoppers, Suffolk region, which is a charity that gathers information regarding crimes from the public anonymously via a call centre in the south of England. The police still live on in my life as I'm in contact with the retired policemen and special constables, unfortunately Mike Robinson and Mike Jarvis have sadly passed away. It is true, police and army life are like being attached to a large family who care for one another, just like freemasonry.

I would like to mention some of the personalities who I worked with me in the Essex Police: - S/Sgt Maurice Mansfield, PC Tony Ward, PC Leslie Carter, PC Ken Marks, Chief Inspector David Le Voire.

Suffolk Constabulary: - Chief Inspector Don Martin, Inspector Murton, S/Insp Mike Robinson MBE, S/Sgt Mick Jarvis, Pc Don Kelly, Sgt Bob Chapman, PC Peter Derrick, SC Ray Fairclough, and many more. I have fond memories of the times spent working with these characters. I joined the forces and then the police for the occasional exciting times to spice up life.

Throughout my life, after a slow start, which may have been due to the blitz or genetics I improved and nearly caught up with my peers. Military service, human resources work, police service and self-employment gave me physical strength, confidence, and cured my gullibility. I still have a hard job with my spelling but I have always been good at composing letters and documents. Having had a secretary helped (I married her) all I had to do was dictate and then check and sign the letters or documents on completion. I may have been slightly dyslexic since an early age which had not detected. I understand these days'problems of this nature are discovered earlier in life.

Me with Brownies for Crime Prevention Event

Result of a life of hard work and fun

I am now fully retired but try to keep active by helping Gladys around the home. I keep driving, because I think if I stopped it would be hard to re-start again.

During my life I've driven many types of vehicle from pre-war cars, many army vehicles from Land Rover Mark 1, buses to heavy recovery vehicles, tanks, armoured cars and all sorts of private cars and light commercial vehicles.

I have been a Freemason since 1980 and belong to Royal Clarence Lodge No. 1823 in Clare, Suffolk and the East & Central Africa Lodge No. 7446 that meets in London, which keeps me in touch with the Swahili language and people from East Africa. I also attend three craft lodges in Saffron Walden Essex on a regular basis in an honorary position of Tyler or Outer Guard. My honorific is PPGJW(Suffolk), LGR(London). Freemasonry helps me to live in peace with myself and my fellows, helping those who have fallen upon hard times throughout the world and ever mindful of the needs of others. I have many masonic friends in Suffolk, Essex, Cambridge Provinces and London Metropolitan Grand Lodge area, a truly large number of what I call my extended family.

On 6th May 2008 I received 'The Honorary Freedom of the Town of Haverhill from the Mayor of Haverhill in recognition of my eminent and courageous service to the Town. I asked the Mayor, "What does this entitle me to." He replied, "You can graze your sheep on the common lands in Haverhill, and walk down the High Street with your sword unsheathed". "I do not have any sheep nor a sword", I replied. It is a great honour and it is good that I have been noticed after many years under the radar.

Receiving 'Freedom of Haverhill'

I have included my family Paternal Tree of the Mackridge Family Tree that stretches back to the 1500's. It always amazes me that the name "Mackridge" has been spelt the same way for nearly four hundred years bearing in mind that people could not always spell correctly in those days. However, there are other names, like Mackrill, Macridge, Mackerth, Mackris and even Achris. It may have been that people could not spell, and names were written down by the parish clerk how the name sounded to him.

I have also been researching my Maternal family tree. My Grandmother whose maiden name was Smith came from a large family, one of her brothers was called Eldon James Smith. born 1864 and died 1936 (a few months before I was born), he was a very successful farmer, builder, constructor and built up a large business empire. His life and business dealings have been recorded by the "Bunwell Heritage Group publications". His son, also Eldon James Smith, born 1895 eventually took over the business and after some time it was run down.

After many years young Eldon James (my great uncle's son) landed up in Perth Australia. While I was serving in the Army living at Nairobi Garrison Kenya, he sent this letter to me: -

"18th December, 1961
c/o Mia Mia
1, Mount Street,
Perth, Western Australia

Dear Eldon,
Thanks for your Xmas card and I wish you all that you would wish yourself for Xmas 1961 and New Year 1962 and all the best of luck.

I thought this would give you a better idea of Western Australia. even to Gold. Just at present there is plenty of work. They are putting in a Wide Gauge Railway costing £40 million and I could easy give you various projects up to a new Harbour Docks etc. £80 million by B.H.P. Ltd. Now they have found oil and many other jobs.
Cheer Oh! & all the best.
Yours etc.
Eldon J. Smith."

This Eldon James Smith, in Australia, seemed to be inviting me to join him. At that time as you may have gathered, I was in the British Army attached to the Army Air Corps and quite content and settled with life at that time.

Most of my forebears were skilled employed or self-employed within their own small companies. A brother of my father Uncle Don John Mackridge born 23rd September, 1909 and died 1st October, 2004 wrote a book in his later years, after researching the Mackridge name most of his life. He didn't have a car in the early days to travel round looking for clues nor a computer, so it must have been an epic and time-consuming job. The book is titled "Seed of Acharis" with a backup quote thus: - "A trip in the North, back to DOMESDAY 1087 from the close of the second MILLENIUM" Don Mackridge has spent many of his retirement years collating various records from the Public Record Office at Kew, the North Yorks Record Office at Northallerton and many other places, all relevant to our Mackridge family background. The book accurately follows the Mackridge family tree back to the 1500's, then after some guess work continues right back to the Normans (1066) This is achieved by studying like sounding names in the same areas. However, Uncle Don does end his book by stating that he may not have interpreted our family tree properly in the dark ages, but he presents a good case for it being correct.

A Story of Luck

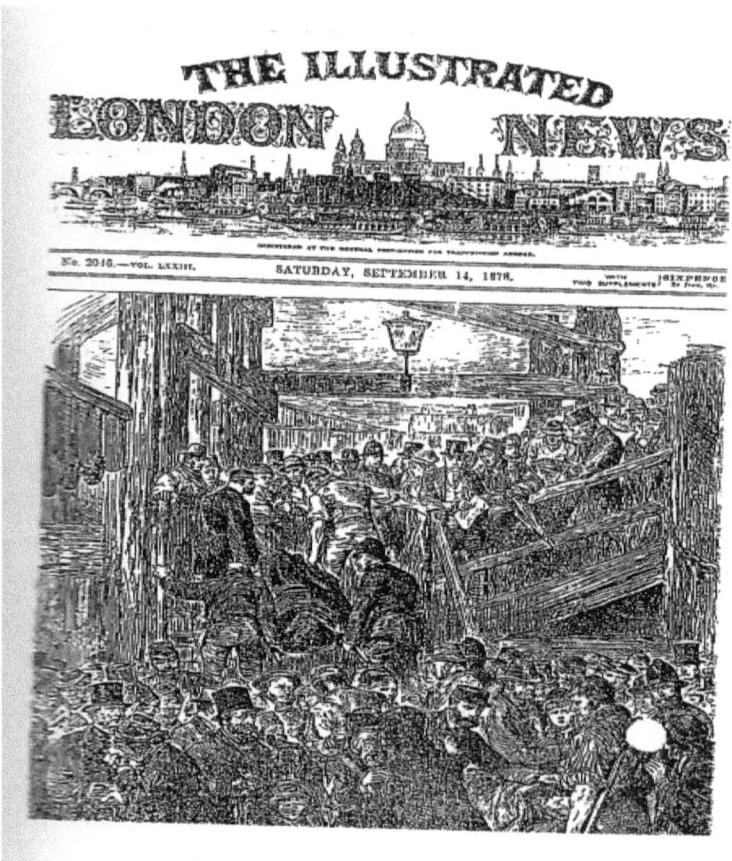

Bringing the dead ashore at Woolwich Pier

With huge kind thanks to my grandfather, my father and Uncle Don John Mackridge for the following. On the 3rd September 1878, my great grandfather John Mackridge decided to take his son, James, my grandfather, on a birthday trip down the River Thames to Sheerness and back. For some unknown reason my great grandfather, John, decided to leave the "Princess Alice" at Woolwich pier and visit Greenwich where they spent the day. It may have been the fact that the boat was very much overloaded. In the late afternoon they returned to Woolwich from Greenwich to wait for the "Princess Alice" on its return journey to London. As they were walking the landing pier they were hailed by the helmsman of a small boat, asking if they were going in the London direction. Instead of waiting for "Princess Alice" they accepted a lift. Without the intervention of this small boat, I would never had come into existence.

The "Princess Alice" was the pride of the London Steamboat Company's fleet of paddle steamers engaged in the river cruise business. It had recently seized the interest of the public due to the fact that the Shah of Persia had a trip on it when he was in London so it became known as the Shah's paddle steamer.

The summer of 1878 had been really hot and September weather continued to bring out the Londoners for a river trip. There were long queues forming early on Tuesday 3rd September eager to get aboard the "Princess Alice" at London Bridge pier for a trip to Gravesend and Sheerness and return. As it embarked at 11:00 hours it was heavily loaded and the directors of the Steamboat Company must have been rubbing their hands with glee.

There was great merriment on board including singing and dancing on the outward journey and also on the return trip that misty evening as it came up Gallion's Reach, near the present London City Airport and Becton gas works area.

The "Bywell Castle" had unloaded its cargo of the Newcastle coal and was coming downstream at this moment. Suddenly the "Princess Alice's" skipper saw the huge steamer issuing from the thick mist. It was too late. Neither captain could at this juncture have given orders which would have avoided a collision. As it transpired the bows of the "Bywell Castle" crashed into the "Princess Alice" amidships cutting it in two and it took a bare twenty minutes for the smaller vessel to go down with its complement of once happy men, women and children. Some, that were on the deck, jumped but there was no escape. Over 600 lives were lost, either by drowning or by asphyxiation in the poisonous waters fed by the waste from a nearby sewage works. This tragedy has never been equalled.

By some freak of providence because my great grandfather John and my grandfather James chose to disembark at Woolwich and spend a day at Greenwich escaped death. Had they remained on board, this story and this book would never been written. Also, many other people alive today would not exist, and YOU would NOT be reading this story now. Creepy, or what.

Most people named "Mackridge" seemed to have traced their roots back to a Ralph Mackridge of Glaisdale in Yorkshire. Here is a tree of the male line back to 1510, some names seem to be Latin. My cousin Peter Mackridge did explain to me on one occasion that it was a possibility that the name Mackridge was an anglicised European name. Females, please do not worry because the complete Family Tree is set out in the later pages. I have researched the names RADULPHUS and GULIELMI. Thus: -
RADULPHUS from Latin "Ralph" meaning "wise wolf".
GULIELMI from French name "William".
These names appear to be correct as Ralph is used in the Tree and William also appears in siblings' names throughout the years.

Direct Family Tree of male Mackridge's
A male and female Family Tree is included in later pages

THOMAS MACKRIDGE born 1510 died?

PETER MACKRIDGE born 1564 died 1602
|
ROGER MACKRIDGE born 1584 died 1636
|
GULIELMI MACKRIDGE born 1600 died???
|
RADULPHUS MACKRIDGE born 1694 died 1762
|
RALPH MACKRIDGE born 1727 died 1808
married MARY FEATHERSTONE born1741 died 1795
|
RALPH MACKRIDGE born 1767 died 1850
married JUDITH LENG b. 1770 m. 1790 died 1836
|
PETER FEATHERSTONE-MACKRIDGE b. 1811 d.1883
married JANE THOMPSON b. 1817 m 1841 d. 1897
|
JOHN MACKRIDGE born 1842 died 1923
married ELIZA THOMPSON b.1840. m.7/8/1871 d.1912
|
JAMES MACKRIDGE b.1/12/1875 d.1/3/1964
married ETHEL MAUD ALICE PURSER b. 1876 m.1899 d.1956

|
JAMES FREDRICK MACKRIDGE b. 22/1/1905 d. 25/12/1986
married EDITH MAY TUNMORE b. 22/2/1901 d. 12/12/1970
|
ELDON JAMES MACKRIDGE born. 8/9/1937
married Gladys Ann SHINN born 20/3/1946 m. 24/2/1968
|
ROBIN ELDON MACKRIDGE born. 18/10/1973
married JACKIE WASHBOURNE b. 6/5/1968 m. 30/3/1996
|three sons
LIAM JAMES MACKRIDGE born 24/8/1996
partner Ellie Simmons
&
RYAN WILLIAM MACKRIDGE born 13 /8/1998
plus
Robin's stepson JAMIE McDonald born 12/9/1989

Family connection with ELDON JAMES SMITH

ELDON JAMES MACKRIDGE b. 8/9/1937   Me.
|Mother
EDITH MAY MACKRIDGE nee TUNMORE b. 22/2/1901
|Grandma
EDITH TUNMORE b. 22/10/1867 d 1949 aged 84 years nee SMITH sister to: - ELDON JAMES SMITH born 1863 died 26th October 1935. aged 72

Therefore, this Eldon James Smith the builder, farmer/contractor was my great uncle. His son also Eldon James Smith contacted me from Perth Western Australia whilst I was in Nairobi. Kenya, East Africa. My mother did take me on a visit to meet this Eldon James at his flat during the 1950's in South London before he left to go to West Australia. On researching the name "Eldon James Smith", with the help of my two daughters Michele May Mackridge b. 13/12/1968 and Lynda Ann Godden nee Mackridge b. 6/10/1971 we uncovered many more Eldon James Smith names from Bunwell, Wymondham, and Deopham Green areas over the 1900 /2000 centuries. Why the names Eldon James was so popular is very strange, I would be grateful to know why. My mother and her grand ideas must have wanted to name me after the more successful members of her family. I have had to live with these names, with pride and honour of those who went before me.

With computers and social media, it is much easier to obtain and exchange information today. It puzzles me how frustrated it must have been for our forebears to even research their grandparents, let alone six or more generations back. However, over the last decades the break down in family relations, by a very few families, has or will form a barrier to future historians to trace their family trees easily. People in the past could not obtain divorce easily so they stayed together for the sake of their children, also it was considered a great sin: - I think due to the vow they made during the marriage ceremony that: - "Those who God has joined together in holy matronly let no man put asunder", must have been in the minds of our ancients. When I started to look at my family's past, I wondered if I'd find a few skeletons in the cupboard. So far, I have not, other than a few bad debts and sons or daughters not continuing their forbears businesses in the correct manner to maintain a good financial return, and therefore losing their family business. We have found birth dates less than nine months after the marriage date, but nothing more sinful than that, so far.

Family Tree

Thomas Mackridge born 1510???
Peter Mackridge born 1564 died 1602
Roger Mackridge born 1584 died 1636
Gulielmi Mackridge born 1600 died?
Radulpus Mackridge born 1694 died 1762?
Ralph Mackridge 1727 died 1808 married Mary Featherstone
Ralph Mackridge 1767 died 1850 married Judith Leng 1779
Peter Featherstone-Mackridge born 1811 died 1883 married Jane Thompson 1841
John Mackridge born 1842 died 1923 married Eliza Thompson
James Mackridge born 1876 died???married Ethel Maud Purser married 28/1/1899
James F. Mackridge born 1905 died 1986 married Edith Tunmore 14/6/1930
Eldon James Mackridge born 8/9/1937 married Gladys Shinn 20/2/1968

Michele Mackridge born 13/12/1968

Lynda Mackridge born 6/10/1971 married Jerry Godden 1/9/1996
Emily Godden born 11/5/2011
Lucy Godden born 28/2/2013

Robin Mackridge born 18/10/1973 married Jackie Washbourn on 30/3/1996
Liam Mackridge born 24/8/1996
Ryan Mackridge born 13/8/1998
Jamie McDonald born 12/9/1990
Jaiden McDonald 30/5/2011

Tunmore section

Thomas Tunmore
Thomas Tunmore born 1827 married Mary Ann King
Charles Tunmore born 8/3/1863 died 9/1938 married Edith Smith born 22/10/1867 died 1949
Brother of Eldon James Smith born 1863 died 26/10/1935 and Bertie Smith.
Edith May Mackridge nee Tunmore born 22/2/1901 died 12/12/1970 my mum.

All the above details and dates are correct as far as I know if you know different, I would be interested to hear.

I may have included some errors in this book unintentional for which I apologise. I am always happy to receive information regarding the stories I have written about and more interestingly ones based on those of my experiences.

Eldon James Mackridge

eldongladys@btinternet.com

Haverhill, Suffolk, England.
July 2021

Milton Keynes UK
Ingram Content Group UK Ltd.
UKHW021113180124
436199UK00008B/27